1 MONTH OF
FREE
READING

at
www.ForgottenBooks.com

By purchasing this book you are eligible for one month membership to ForgottenBooks.com, giving you unlimited access to our entire collection of over 700,000 titles via our web site and mobile apps.

To claim your free month visit:
www.forgottenbooks.com/free445272

ISBN 978-0-483-98245-1
PIBN 10445272

A
DISCOURSE
Proving The
Divine Inſtitution
OF
𝕬𝖆𝖙𝖊𝖗 - 𝕭𝖆𝖕𝖙𝖎𝖘𝖒 :
Wherein The
Quaker-Arguments
Againſt it, Are
COLLECTED and CONFUTED.
With as much as is Needful concerning
𝕿𝖍𝖊 𝕷𝖔𝖗𝖉'𝖘 𝕾𝖚𝖕𝖕𝖊𝖗.

By the *Author* of, *The Snake in the Graſs.*

If ye Love me, keep my Commandments, Joh. xiv. 15.

L·O N D O N :

Printed for *C. Brome*, at the *Gun*, at the *Weſt-End* of St. *Pauls.*
W. Keblewhite, at the *White Swan*, in St. *Pauls Church-Yard.*
And *H. Hindmarſh*, at the *Golden Ball*, over-againſt the
Royal Exchange, in *Cornhill*. M.DC.XC.VII.

THE

PREFACE

CONTAINS.

The Contents *of This* Difcourfe.

Erratum. P. 5. l. 14. r. *Act.* x. 47.

There will foon be Publiſhed a *Diſcourſe,* by the fame *Author,* ſhewing whom *Chriſt* hath *Ordained* to *Adminiſter* the *Sacraments* in His *Church.* And another, wherein it is prov'd, That the Chief of the *Quaker-Hereſies* were *Broached,* and *Condemned,* in the Days of the *Apoſtles,* and in the firſt 150 Years after *Chriſt.*

A PREFACE.

AS Baptiſm *is putting on* Chriſt, *giving up our Names to Him* ; *bei* *Admitted as His* Diſciples ; *and a* Publick Profeſſion *of His* D ⳑrin : *So the Renouncing of our* Baptiſm, *is as* Publick *a* Diſow ing *of Him* ; *and a Formal* Apoſtaſy *from His* Religion.

Therefore *the* Devil *has been moſt buſie in all ages* (*but has p* *vailed moſt, in our latter Corrupt times*) *to Prejudice Men, by many f* Pretences, *againſt this* Divine Inſtitution. *Having been able to perſwade ſo* *quite to throw it off, as* Pernicious *and* Hurtful *: Others to think it o* *ly* Lawful *to be done, but to lay no great ſtreſs upon it, and ſo uſe it, whe* *it is Enjoined, as a thing* Indifferent. *Others deny it to* Infants, *up* *this only Ground, That they are not ſuppos'd Capable of being Admitted in* *the* Covenant *of God, which He has made with Men : For, if they are Cap* *ble of being admitted into the* Covenant, *there can be no Reaſon to de* *them the outward* Seal *of it.*

But *this being* Foreign *to my preſent* Undertaking, *which is to* D *monſtrate to the* Quakers *the Neceſſity of an* Outward *or* Water-Baptiſm *in the* General (*for as to Perſons capable of it, we have no Controve* *ſie with thoſe who deny it to* All) *therefore, I have not digreſs'd into an* *ther Subjeⳑ, which is, that of* Infant Baptiſm, *in the following* Diſcourſ

I. Yet *thus much I will ſay of it, in this place, That* Infants *are Capable* *being admitted into the* Covenant, *and therefore that they cannot be Exclude* *from the outward* Seal *of it. The Conſequence the* Baptiſts *cannot deny. An* *that they are Capable, I thus prove. They were Capable under the* Law, *an* *before the* Law, *of being admittted as Members of the* Covenant *in* Chriſt *come, made with* Abraham, *by the Seal of* Circumciſion, *at the Age of* Eigh Days *: And therefore there can be no Reaſon to Exclude them from the ſam* *Privilege, to the ſame* Covenant, *now that* Chriſt *is come ; unleſs* Chriſt *ha* *debarr'd them from it : The Law ſtanding ſtill, as it was, where He has n* Alter'd, *or* Fulfill'd *it. But He has not debarr'd them. Nay, on the contrary, H* *has yet further confirm'd their being within the* Covenant. *He called a* Li tle Child, (Mat. xviii. 2, 3, 5.) *and ſet him in the midſt of His* Apoſtles ; *an* *Propoſed him as a* Pattern *to* Them, *and to all* Adult Chriſtians *: And ſaid, Th* *none ſhould* enter into the Kingdom of Heaven, *except thoſe who ſhoul* become as little Children. *And that whoever did Receive a* Little Child *i* His Name, *did Receive* Chriſt Himſelf. *And* (ver 10.) *in Heaven, thei* Angels (*ſaith* Chriſt) do always behold the Face of my Father which is i Heaven. *And therefore He bids us* Take heed that we deſpiſe not one of the

A Preface.

not been *Adminiſtred till the Reſtauration*, 1660, *that is, in ſome Churches for* Ten, *in*
ſe for Twelve *Years together.*

V. *Theſe* Presbyterians *in* Dublin, *and in the South and Weſt parts of* Ireland, *were ſent*
in England, *and had learnt the Contempt of this Sacrament there.* Where, *even in* Ox-
d, it was not Adminiſtred *in the whole* Univerſity, *from the Ejection of the* Epiſcopal
ergy, *in the Year* 1648. *to the Reſtauration in* 1660, *as is obſerved in the* Antiquit.
xon. *So that the* Quakers *have only taken that out of the way, which the* Presbyterians
d worn into Diſ-uſe.

VI. *And from all theſe Enemies, and the ſubtle Inſinuations which they have broached in*
ejudice of Chriſt's *Holy Inſtitution of* Baptiſm, *and likewiſe of the* Lords Supper *(for*
h are ſlighted by the ſame Perſons, and upon the ſame Grounds) it is to be feared, that ſeve-
l, even of the Church of England, *have been wrought, tho' not into a* Diſ-uſe, *or downright*
ght, yet into a leſs Eſteem, *and greater* Indifferency *as to theſe* Holy Sacraments *than*
y ought ; and conſequently receive leſs Benefit by them ; much leſs than if their Knowledge,
d their Faith *were better rooted, and more ſublime. Nay, there is not any Degree of* indif-
ency, but what is Culpable, in this Caſe ; and may bring a Curſe *with it, inſtead of a*
eſſing : for, whatſoever, eſpecially in Religious *Worſhip, is not of* Faith, *is* ſin. *And*
ording to our Faith, *it is to us, in all our Performances of* Religion.

VII. *For all theſe Reaſons, tho' this Diſcourſe was wrote wholly on Behalf of the* Quakers,
, I hope, it will not be un-uſeful to many others, to ſee the ſtrong Foundation, Great Ne-
ſity, and In-eſtimable Benefits of Baptiſm *and the* Lord's Supper, *when Duly Admini-*
'd, and Receiv'd with Full Faith *and* Aſſurance *in the* Power *and* Love *of* God, *that*
will not fail to aſſiſt His own Inſtitutions, *when we approach unto them, with ſincere* Re-
ntance, and undoubting Dependance upon His Promiſes. *And many of the Objections*
ſeafter anſwered, tho' uſed by the Quakers, *to* Invalidate BAPTISM, *are likewiſe inſiſted*
by ſeveral of the Sects, *which I have named above, to* Leſſen *and* Diſparage *it. In which*
ſe, the following Diſcourſe, tho' it reſpects the QUAKERS *Chiefly, yet not them* Only,
it contains the joint Arguments of all the ſeveral ſizes of the Oppoſers, *or* Contemners
Baptiſm.

VIII. *But as to the immediate Occaſion, which engaged me in this Work, it was upon the*
count of a particular Perſon, who had been Educated *from his Childhood in the* Quaker
inciples, and Communion. And the Objections which are here conſidered againſt Baptiſm,
theſe which, at ſeveral conferences with other Quakers, *to whom that Perſon brought me,*
re inſiſted upon. At length, after more than Twelve Months *conſideration of this ſingle*
nt, and diligently Reading *over, and weighing every particular, which* Rob. Barclay *had*
ate, in his Apology, *againſt the* Outward, *or* Water Baptiſm, *it pleaſed* God *ſo to open*
Eyes, *and perſwade the Heart of this Gentleman, that, having Informed himſelf in the*
e Principles of the Chriſtian *Religion, as contained in our* Church Catechiſm ; *he has*
ly with great joyfulneſs, and ſatisfaction, Received the Baptiſm *of* Chriſt, *as Admini-*
d in the Church of England. *And it was his Deſire, that this* Diſcourſe *(tho' wrote for*
Privat Uſe) might be made Publick, *in hopes, that it may have the like Effects upon others,*
t has had upon himſelf, by the great Mercy *of* God. *And I knowing ſeveral others who*
re of late been Convinced *and* Baptiſed, *in the ſame manner, as this Gentleman ; I have*
Reſiſted his invitation to contribute my Mite *towards the Recovery of ſo many* Thouſand
s as now for 46 *years, have thrown off the* Sacraments *of* Chriſt's Inſtitution : *and there-*
as one main Cauſe, have loſt the Subſtance, even Faith *in the Blood of* Chriſt, *outwardly*
for our Salvation, *as I have elſe-where ſhewn. The* Lord *accept my mean Endeavours ;*
make them Inſtrumental to His Glory, *and the Salvation of Souls.* Amen.

A DISCOURSE,

PROVING

The DIVINE INSTITUTION

OF

WATER-BAPTISM.

SECT. I.

That Matth. xxviii. 19. *was meant of* Water-Baptism.

THE Words of the Text are these: *Go ye, therefore, and Teach all Nations, Baptizing them in the Name of the Father, and of the Son, and of the Holy Ghost.*

The *Quakers* will not own that the *Baptism* here mentioned was the *Outward*, or *Water-baptism*: Which I will endeavour to make very plain, that it was; and that in the first place, From the *Signification* and *Etymology* of the word *Baptize*.

1. The word is a *Greek* word, and only made *English* by our constant usage of it: It signifies to *Wash*, and is apply'd to this *Sacrament* of *Baptism*, because that is an outward *Washing*.

To *Wash* and to *Baptize* are the very same; and if the word *Baptize* had been rendred into *English*, instead of, *Go and* BAPTIZE, it must have been said, *Go and* WASH *Men, in the Name of the Father, and of the Son, and of the Holy Ghost*. So that the outward *Baptism*, with *Water*, is as much here commanded, as if it had been expressed in *English* words, or as we can now express it.

B   But

But becaufe the word *Baptize* was grown a Technical Term, in other Languages, whereby to exprefs the Holy Sacrament of *Baptifm,*long before our *Erglifh* Tranflation,therefore our Tranfators did rightly retain the word *Baptize* in this Text, *Matth.* xxviii. 19. and in other Texts which fpeak of that *Holy Sacrament.*

But in other places they tranflate the word *Baptize,* as *Mark* vii. 4. *When they come from the Market* ἐὰν μὴ Βαπίἴσωνται, except they are *Baptized,* which we literally tranflate except they *Wafh.* And in the fame Verfe, Βαπίἴσμὸς ποτηρίων, &c. The *Baptifms* of *Cups* and *Pots,* &c. which we tranflate the *Wafhing* of *Cups* and *Pots.* And *Heb.* ix. 10. fpeaking of thefe Legal Inftitutions, *which ftood only in Meats and Drinks, and divers Wafhings, and carnal Ordinances,* &c. the word which we here tranflate *Wafhings,* is, in the Original, Βαπίἴσμοῖς, *Baptifms : In Meats and Drinks, and divers Baptifms.* And in the *Vulgar Latin,* the *Greek* word is retained in both thefe Texts, Mark vii. 4. *Nifi Baptizentur, non Comedunt.* Except they are *Baptized, i. e. Wafh* their *Hands,* they eat not. And *Baptifmata Calicum,* &c. The *Baptifms* of *Cups,* &c. And *Heb.* ix. 10. *In Cibis & Potibus, & variis Baptifmatibus ; i. e. In Meats and Drinks, and divers Baptifms.* So that it is plain that the word *Baptifm,* and the word *Wafhing,* tho' not the fame word, have yet the felf-fame meaning.

2. It is true, that the word *Baptifm* is often taken in a *Figurative* and *Allegorical* Senfe, to mean the INWARD BAPTISM, the *Wafhing,* or *Cleanfing* of the *Heart :* But fo is the word *Wafhing* alfo, as often, as *Jer.* iv.14, &c. And there is fcarce a Word in the World but is capable of many *Figurative* and *Allegorical* Meanings. Thus *Circumcifion* is very often us'd for the *Inward Circumcifion* or *Purity* of the *Heart.* And *Fire* is taken to exprefs *Love,* and likewife *Anger,* and many other things.

But it is a receiv'd Rule for the Interpretation of *Scripture,* and indeed of all other *Writings* and *Words,* that the plain *Literal* Meaning is always to be taken, where there is no manifeft *Contradiction* or *Abfurdity* in it ; as when a Man is faid to have a *Fire* burning in his *Breaft,* it cannot be meant of the *Literal Fire :* fo when we are commanded to *Wafh* or *Circumcife* our

Hearts, and the like. But, on the other hand, if any Man will take upon him to underſtand Words in a *Figurative Senſe*, at his own will and pleaſure,. without an apparent Neceſſity from the *Scope* and *Coherence*, he ſets up to *Banter*, and leaves no *Certainty* in any *Words* or *Expreſſions* in the World. Therefore I will conclude this Point of the natural *Signification* and *Etymology* of the word *Baptize*: And, unleſs the *Quakers* can ſhew an apparent *Contradiction* or *Abſurdity* to take it in the *Literal Signification*, in this Text, *Matth.* xxviii. 19. then it muſt be meant of the OUTWARD WASHING or BAPTISM, becauſe that is the only *True*, and *Proper*, and *Literal* Signification of the Word.

And it will be further Demonſtrated in the next *Section*, that there can be no *Contradiction* or *Abſurdity* to take it in a *Literal* Senſe, becauſe the *Apoſtles*, and Others thereunto *Commiſſionated* by them, did Practiſe it, in the *Literal* Senſe.

S E C T. II.

I. *That* C H R I S T *did Practiſe* Water-Baptiſm. II. *That the Apoſtles did it after* Him. III. *That the* Catholick Church *have done it after* Them.

I. THat *Chriſt* did Practiſe *Water-Baptiſm.* It is written, *John* iii. 26. *And they came unto John, and ſaid unto him, Rabbi, He that was with thee beyond Jordan, to whom thou bareſt witneſs, Behold, the ſame Baptizeth, and all Men come to Him.*

That this was *Water-Baptiſm* there can be no Doubt, becauſe,

1. The *Baptiſm with the Holy Ghoſt* was not yet given: For that was not given till the Day of *Pentecoſt*, fifty Days after the *Reſurrection* of *Chriſt*, as it is Recorded in the Second of the *Acts.* This *Spiritual Baptiſm* was promiſed, *John* xiv. 16, 26. xv. 26. xvi. 7. And the *Apoſtles* were commanded to tarry in the City of *Jeruſalem* till it ſhould come upon them, *Luke* xxiv. 49. 2. The *Quakers* allow that *John* did *Baptize* with *Water*, and there is no other ſort of *Baptiſm* here mentioned, with

which

which *Christ* did *Baptize* ; and therefore, thefe *Baptifms* being fpoke of both together, there can be no Reafon to interpret the *one* to be with *Water*, and the *other* not. It is faid *John* iv. 1. *The Pharifees heard that Jefus made and baptized more Difciples than John.* How cou'd the *Pharifees* hear of it, if it was not an *Outward* and *Vifible Baptifm* ? For, as before is faid, the *outward* and *miraculous* Effects of the *Baptifm with the Holy Ghoft* were not then given. And fince it Was an *Outward*, it muft be the *Water-baptifm*, for there was *then* no other.

Obj. But the *Quakers* ftart an *Objection* here, That it is faid *John* iv. 2. *Jefus himfelf baptized not, but his Difciples.*

1. *Anf.* Tho *Jefus himfelf baptized not*, yet it is faid in the *Verfe* foregoing, that *He made* and *baptized*, i. e. thofe whom *His Difciples*, by His Order, *Baptized.* For, if it had not been done *by His Order*, it cou'd not be faid that he had *Baptized* thofe whom his Difciples *Baptized.* But becaufe, *He that doeth a thing by Another*, is faid to *do it Himfelf*, therefore *Chrift* himfelf is faid to have *Baptized* thofe, whom his Difciples, by his Order, did *Baptize.*

2. *Anfw.* That *Baptizing* which *Chrift* is faid to have Adminiftred *himfelf*, *John* iii. 26. might have been at another *Time* than that which is mentioned in the 4th *Chapter* : And then the confequence will only be this, That, at *fome Times*, *Chrift* did Baptife *Himfelf* ; and at *other Times*, he left it to his *Difciples.* Tho, as to our Argument, it is the fame thing, whether he did it *Himfelf*, or commanded his *Difciples* to do it. For, either way, it is *his Baptifm, his Onely* ; his *Difciples* did but *Adminifter* what he commanded.

II. As *Chrift* himfelf did *Baptize* with *Water*, and his *Difciples*, by his Commandment, while he was with them upon Earth ; fo did his *Apoftles*, and Others thereunto by them commiffionated, after his *Death*, and *Refurrection*, by vertue of his Command to them, *Matth.* xxviii. 19. after he was Rifen from the Dead.

What is faid above of the *Etymology* and true *Signification* of the word *Baptize*, is, of itfelf, fufficient to prove, that by *Baptifm* in this *Text*, the *outward Baptifm* with *Water* is meant : efpecially till the *Quakers* can fhew any *Contradiction* or *Abfurdity* in having the word taken in the *proper* and *literal* fenfe, in this, and the other *Texts* which fpeak of it.   And

And this will be very hard to do, since, as it is juſt now proved, that *Chriſt* did *Baptize* with *Water*, as well as *John*. And what *Abſurdity*, or *Contradiction* can be alledged, that his *Apoſtles* ſhou'd Adminiſter the ſame ſort of *Baptiſm*, after his *Death*, as he had *Practiſed* and Commanded during his *Life* ? Nay rather, what Reaſon can be given, why they ſhou'd not be the ſame, ſince the ſame *word*, i. e. *Baptize*, is us'd in Both, and no new *Senſe* or *Acceptation* of the *word* is ſo much as hinted ? And therefore to put any new *ſenſe* or *acceptation* of the *word*, muſt be wholly *Arbitrary* and *Precarious*.

But, as I promis'd, I will Demonſtrate yet more fully and plainly, that the *Apoſtles* did *Practiſe* the *Outward*, i. e. *Water-Baptiſm* after CHRIST's death.

Acts x. 47. *Can any Man forbid* Water, *that theſe ſhou'd not be Baptized ?*

Acts viii. 36. *As they* (Philip *and the* Eunuch) *went on their way, they came to a certain* Water, *and the Eunuch ſaid, See here is* Water, *what doth hinder me to be Baptized?* —*And* (Verſe 38.) *they went both down into the* Water, *both Philip and the Eunuch, and he Baptized him : And when they were come up out of the* WATER, &c.

Acts xxii. 16. *And now why tarrieſt thou ? Ariſe and be Baptized, and* waſh *away thy ſins*.

And, to ſave more Quotations, the *Quakers* do own that the *Baptiſm* of the *Corinthians*, mentioned 1 *Cor.* i. 14 & 17. was *Water-baptiſm*.

Therefore I will conclude this Point, as undeniable, That the *Apoſtles* did practiſe *Water-baptiſm*.

And the Argument from thence will lie thus : The *Apoſtles* did practiſe that *Baptiſm* which *Chriſt* commanded *Mat.* xxviii. 19. But the *Apoſtles* did practiſe *Water-baptiſm* ; therefore *Water-baptiſm* was that *Baptiſm* which *Chriſt* commanded *Matth.* xxviii. 19.

III. And, as the *Practiſe* of the *Apoſtles* is a moſt ſure Rule whereby to underſtand the meaning of that *Command* which they put in *execution* ; ſo the *Practiſe* of thoſe who immediately ſucceeded the *Apoſtles*, who were Cotemporaries with them, and learn'd the Faith from their Mouths, is as certain a Rule to know what the *Practiſe*, and what the *Senſe* of the *Apoſtles* were.

were. And thus the *Practife* of the *prefent Age*, in the Admini-ftration of *Water-baptifm*, is an undeniable Evidence, that this was the *Practife* of the *laft Age*; the fame Perfons being, many of them, alive in both the *laft* and the *prefent Age*. For one *Age* does not go off the World all at once, and another fucceed all of *perfect Age* together; but there are *old Men* of the *laft Age*, and *young Men* and *Children* growing up to another *Age* all alive up-on Earth the fame time; and *Mankind* being difperfed into far diftant *Countries* and *Climates*, who know not of one another, nor hold any Correfpondence: It is, by thefe means, morally impoffible for any *Man* or *Men*, to deceive us in what has been the *Univerfal* and Receiv'd *Practife* of the *laft Age*, to which the *prefent Age* is fo linked, that it is even a part of it: I fay it is impoffible for *all* the *Fathers* of the World, to be fuppos'd *wil-ling*, or if they were, to be *capable* of impofing upon all *younger* than themfelves, namely, That they had been all *Baptized*, and that this was an univerfally receiv'd *Cuftom*; and of which *Regi-fters* were always kept, in every *Parifh*, of *all* who had been, from time to time, *Baptized*; and that fuch *Regifters* were *publick*, and to be recurr'd to by all that had a mind to it: Every Man's rea-fon will tell him that it is utterly impoffible for fuch a thing to pafs upon Mankind.

And as certainly as the *prefent Age* is thus affur'd of the *Pra-ctife* of the *laft Age*, in a Thing of fo *publick* and *univerfal* a na-ture; fo certainly, and by the fame Rules, muft the *laft Age* know the *Practife* of the *Age* before that; and fo backward all the way to the *firft Inftitution*, to the *Age* of *Chrift*, and the *A-poftles*.

The *publick* nature of this *Water-baptifm*, as now practifed, being an *outward* matter of *Fact*, of which Mens *outward Senfes*, their *Eyes* and *Ears* are *Judges*; not like Matters of *Opinion*, which fort of *Tares* may be *privately* fown, and *long time* propa-gated, without any remarkable Difcovery; And to this fo *pub-lick* matter of *Fact*, adding the *univerfal* Practice of it, through all the far diftant Nations of *Chriftianity*: I fay thefe two *Marks* make it impoffible for the World to be impos'd upon, nor was it ever, or ever can be impos'd upon, in any fuch *publick* Matter of *Fact*, fo *univerfally* practifed. All this makes it undeniably plain, That the *laft Age* did *practife* the fame *outward Water-ba-*

ptifm

ptifm which is practis'd in *this Age*; and that the same was, as certainly, practis'd in the *Age* before the *last Age*, and by the same Rule, in the *Age* before that; and so onward, as abovesaid, to the *Age* of the *Apoftles*. I have made more Words of this than needed, but I wou'd render it exceeding plain, considering with whom I have to do. And I beseech them to consider, That all the Authority which they have to Over-ballance all these Demonftrations, is the mad *Enthufiafm* of a *Lay-Apoftle*, *George Fox*, a *Mechanick* so *Illiterate*, that he was hardly Mafter of *common Senfe*, nor cou'd write *English*, or any other Language; and ftarted up amongft us in the Year 1650, (the Age of *Schifm* and *Rebellion*) and Damn'd, as *Apoftates*, all *Ages* fince the *Apoftles*.

In all of which no One cou'd be found (before *G. Fox*) to bear their Teftimony againft this *Water-baptifm*, tho' it was *conftantly* and *univerfally* practifed; and that *Chriftians* were then so *Zealous* as to contend againft the leaft Variation or Corruption of the *Faith*, even unto *Death*, and the moft cruel fort of *Martyrdom*.

Can any Man imagin, that if *Water-baptifm* were a *Human Invention*, or *Superftitiously* either *Continu'd* or *Obtruded* upon the *Church*, no One fhou'd be found, for 1650 Years, to open his Mouth againft it; when *Thoufands* facrific'd their *Lives*, for Matters of much lefs Importance?

But I have over-labour'd this Point, to any Man who will give himfelf leave to make ufe of his Reafon. Therefore I will proceed to the next *Section*.

SECT. III.

That Baptifm *muft be* Outward *and* Vifible, *becaufe it is an Ordinance appointed whereby to* Initiate *Men into an* Outward *and* Vifible *Society, which is the* Church.

THere goes no more towards the proving of this, than to fhew, 1ft, That the *Church* is an *Outward* and *Vifible Society*. 2dly, That *Baptifm* was appointed and us'd for *Initiating* or *Admitting* Men into the *Church*.

1ft,

1ft, That the *Church* is an *outward* and *vifible* Society. Our *Saviour* calls it, *A City that is fet on a Hill,* (Matth. v. 14.) The *Quakers* themfelves are an *outward* and *vifible Society*; and fo are all thofe who bear the Name of *Churches* upon Earth. They cou'd not otherwife be *Churches*. For that implies a *Society* of *People*; and every *Society* in the World, is an *outward* and *vifible* Thing.

And, as it is fo, has an *outward* and *vifible Form* of Admitting Men into it: For otherwife it wou'd not be known who are *Members* of it. Every *Society* is *Exclufive* of all others who are not of that *Society*; otherwife it cou'd not be a *Society*: for that fuppofes the Men of that *Society*, to be thereby diftinguifhed from other Men: And that fuppofes as much that there muft be fome *outward* and *vifible* Form whereby to *Initiate* Men, and intitle them to be *Members* of fuch a *Society*: otherwife it cou'd not be known who were *Members* of it, and who were not; and it wou'd thereby *ipfo facto* ceafe to be a *Society*; for it cou'd not then be diftinguifhed from the reft of Mankind: as a *River* is loft in the *Sea*, becaufe it is no longer diftinguifh'd from it, but goes to make up a part of it.

From hence it appears, that the *Church*, being an *outward* and *vifible Society*, muft have fome *outward* and *vifible Form* to initiate Men, and make them *Members* of that *Society*.

2dly, That *Baptifm* was that *outward Form*. All the feveral *Baptifms* that were before *Chrift's*, were all meant for *Initiating Forms*. The *Jews* had a Cuftom long before *Chrift*, to *initiate* the *Profelites* or *Converts* to their Religion, not only by *Circumcifion*, but by *Baptizing*, or *Wafhing* them with *Water*. The fame was the meaning of *John's Baptifm*, to make Men his *Difciples*. And the fame was the meaning of *Chrift's Baptifm*, to *initiate* Men into the *Chriftian Religion*, and make them *Difciples* of *Chrift*.

Hence *Baptizing* Men, and making them *Difciples*, mean the fame thing. Thus *John* iv. 1. it is faid, That *Jefus made and baptized more Difciples than John*. That is, be *baptized* them *Difciples*, which was the *Form* of *Making* them fuch. If any will fay, that he *baptized* them to be *Difciples* to *John*, that will be anfwer'd Sect. VI. But as to the prefent Point, it is the fame thing

thing whose *Disciples* they were made ; for we are now only to shew that *Baptism*, in the general, was an *Initiating Form*.

And when *Christ* practised it, as well as *John*, as this Text does expresly declare, no Reason can be given that he did not use it as an *Initiating Form*, as well as *John* ; especially when the Text does expres that he did *make* them *Disciples*, by *baptizing* of them, as above is shewn.

And pursuant to this, when *Christ* sent his *Apostles* to convert *all Nations*, his Commission of *Baptizing* was as large as that of *Teaching*, Matth. xxviii. 19. *Go* Teach *all Nations*, Baptizing *them*, &c. *i. e. Baptizing* all who shall receive your word. And accordingly it is said, *Acts* ii. 41. *They that received the word were baptized.* Pursuant to what the *Apostle* had preached to them *Verse* 28. *Repent and be baptized.*

And accordingly we find it the constant Custom to *baptize* all that were converted to the *Faith.* Thus *Paul*, tho *miraculously* converted from *Heaven*, was commanded to be *baptized*, Acts xxii. 16. And he *baptized Lydia*, and the *Jaylor*, and their Households, as soon as he had converted them, *Acts* xvi. 15, 33. And the *Corinthians*, Acts xviii. 8. And the *Disciples* of *John*, who had not yet been made *Christians*, Acts xix. 5. *Philip* did *baptize* the *Eunuch*, as soon as he believed in *Christ*, Acts viii. 37, 38. And *Peter*, immediately upon the Conversion of *Cornelius*, and those with him, said, *Can any Man forbid Water, that these shou'd not be baptized ?* Acts x. 47.

It wou'd be endless to enumerate all the like Instances of *Baptism*, in the *New Testament*. And it was always us'd as an *Initiating Form*.

3dly, *Baptism* was not only an *Initiating Form :* But it serv'd for nothing else. For it was never to be *repeated*. As a Man can be *born* but *once* into this World; so he can be but *once regenerated*, or *born* into the *Church*; which is therefore, in *Scripture*, called the *New Birth*.

It is said of the other Sacrament (of the *Lord's Supper*) *as often as ye eat this Bread*, &c. I Cor. xi. 26. This was to be *often* repeated.

Baptism is our *Admission, Initiation*, or *Birth* into the *Society* of the *Church*; and accordingly *once only* to be administred. The

C

Lord's Supper is our *Nourishment* and *Daily Food* in it; and there- fore to be *often* repeated.

And as of our *Saviour's*, so of other *Baptisms*, of *John's*, and the *Jews*, they being only *Initiating Forms*, they were not re- peated. The *Jews* did not *baptize* their *Proselites* more than *once*. And *John* did not *baptize* his *Disciples* more than *once*. So neither were Men *twice baptized* into the *Christian Faith*, more than they were *twice Circumcised*, or *Admitted* into the *Church*, be- fore *Christ*.

Thus having proved, 1st, That the *Church* is an *outward* and *visible* Society. 2dly, That *Baptism* was the *Initiating Form* of *Admitting* Men into that *Society*. 3dly, That it was only an *Initiating Form*. I think the Consequence is undeniable, that this *Baptism* must be an *outward* and *visible Form* : Becauſe other- wise it cou'd be no *Sign* or *Badge* of an Admiſſion into an *outward* and *visible* Society; for ſuch a *Badge* muſt be as *outward* as the Society.

Again, Acts of *inward Faith* are, and ought to be *often repeat- ed* : Therefore this *Baptism*, which cou'd not be *repeated*, cou'd not be the *inward*, but the *outward* Baptiſm.

And thus having prov'd *that Baptism* commanded *Matth.* xxviii. 19. to be the *outward*, that is, *Water-baptism* : 1ſt, From the *true* and *proper Etymology* and *Signification* of the *Word*. 2dly, From the *Practise* of Christ, and his *Apostles*, and the whole *Christian Church* after them. And, 3dly, From the Na- ture of the *Thing*, *Baptism* being an Ordinance appointed only for *Initiating* Men into an *outward* and *visible Society*; and therefore never to be *repeated* : Having thus prov'd our Conclusion from ſuch plain, eaſie, and certain Topicks ; I will now proceed to thoſe Objections (ſuch as they are) which the *Quakers* do ſet up againſt all theſe clear Demonſtrations. And ſhall according- ly, in the firſt place, take notice of their *groundleſs Pretence* in making *that* Baptism commanded in the *Holy Goſpel*, and pro- ved an Ordinance *external* and *visible*, to be underſtood only or the *Inward* and *Spiritual* Baptism, not with Water, but the Holy Ghost.

SECT.

SECT. IV.

Quakers *fay*, 1ft, *That the* BAPTISM *commanded* Matth. xxviii. 19. *was only meant of the* Inward *and* Spiritual *Baptifm*, with the Holy Ghoft.

THey *fay* this; and that is all. They neither pretend to *anfwer* the *Arguments* brought againft them, fuch as thefe before-mentioned; nor give any *Proof* for their own *Affertion.* Only they *fay fo*; and they *will* believe it; and there is an End of it.

And truly there fhou'd be an End of it, if only *Difputation*, or *Victory* were my Defign: For to what *non plus* can any Adverfary be reduc'd beyond that of neither *Anfwering*, nor *Proving?*

But becaufe the Pains I have taken is only in Charity for their Souls, I will over-look all their Impertinency, and deal with them as with weyward Children, humour them, and follow them thro' all their *Windings* and *Turnings*; and fubmit to *over-prove*, what is abundantly *proved* already. Therefore, fince they can give no Reafon why *that Baptifm* commanded *Matth.* xxviii. 19. fhou'd be meant *only* of the *Baptifm* with the *Holy Ghoft*; and wou'd be content that we fhou'd leave them there, as obftinate Men, and purfue them no further; but let them perfwade thofe whom they can perfwade: By which Method (unhappily yielded to them) they have gain'd and fecur'd moft of their *Profelites*, by keeping them from *Difputing* or *Reafoning*; and by perfwading them to hearken only to their own *Light within*: To Refcue them out of this Snare, I will be content to undertake the *Negative* (though againft the Rules of Argument,) and to prove, that the *Baptifm* commanded *Matth.* xxviii. 19. was not the *Baptifm* with the *Holy Ghoft.* For,

1ft, To *baptize* with the *Holy Ghoft* is peculiar to *Chrift* alone. For none can *baptize* with the *Holy Ghoft*, but who can *fend* and *beftow* the *Holy Ghoft.* Which is *Blafphemy* to afcribe to any Creature. C 2 *Chrift*

Christ has indeed committed the Adminiſtration of the *outward Baptiſm* with *Water* to his *Apoſtles*, and to Others by them thereunto *ordained*; and has promiſed the *inward Baptiſm* of the *Holy Ghoſt* to thoſe who ſhall *duly* receive the *outward Baptiſm*.

But this cannot give the *Apoſtles*, or any other *Miniſters* of *Christ*, the Title of *baptizing* with the *Holy Ghoſt*; though the *Holy Ghoſt* may be given by their *Miniſtration*. For they are not the *Givers*; that is *Blaſphemy*.

And purſuant to this, it is obſervable, that none is ever ſaid, in the *Scripture*, to *baptize with the Holy Ghoſt* but *Christ* alone: *The ſame is he who baptizeth with the Holy Ghoſt*, John i. 33.

And therefore, if that *Baptiſm* commanded *Matth.* xxviii. 19. was the *Baptiſm* with the *Holy Ghoſt*, it wou'd follow that the *Apoſtles* cou'd *baptize* with the *Holy Ghoſt*, which is *Blaſphemy* to aſſert.

2dly, It is written, *John* iv. 2. That *Jeſus himſelf baptized not, but his Diſciples.* If this was not meant of *Water-baptiſm*, but of the *Baptiſm* with the *Holy Ghoſt*; then it will follow, That *Christ* did *not baptize* with the *Holy Ghoſt*, but that his *Diſciples* did.

This, in ſhort, may ſuffice in return to a *meer Pretence*, and proceed we next to conſider, if their *main Argument* alſo prove as unſupported and precarious.

SECT. V.

The great Argument of the Quakers *againſt* Water-Baptiſm *is this:* John's Baptiſm *is* ceaſed: *But* John's Baptiſm *was* Water-Baptiſm: *Therefore* Water-Baptiſm *is* ceaſed. *This their Learned* Barclay *makes uſe of.* But,

1ſt, IT is ſo extreamly *Childiſh*, that if it were not *His*, no *Reader* wou'd Pardon me for Anſwering to it. Yet ſince they do inſiſt upon it, let them take this eaſie Anſwer: That *John's*

John's *Water-baptifm* is *ceafed*; but not *Chriſt's Water-baptiſm.* All *outward Baptiſms* were *Water-baptiſms*, as the word *Baptiſm* fignifies, *(See* Sect. I.) The *Jews Baptiſm* was *Water-baptiſm*, as well as *John*'s. And by this Argument of *Barclay*'s, the *Jews* and *John*'s may be prov'd to be the fame. Thus. The *Jews Baptiſm* was *Water-baptiſm*: but *John*'s *Baptiſm* was *Water-baptiſm*: therefore *John*'s *Baptiſm* was the *Jews Baptiſm*.

And thus, *Chriſt's Baptiſm* was *John*'s, and *John*'s was the *Jews*, and the *Jews* was *Chriſt's*; and they were *all* one and the felf-fame *Baptiſm*, becaufe they were all *Water-baptiſms*.

So without all Foundation is this great Rock of the *Quakers*, upon which they build their main Battery againft *Water-baptiſm*.

2ly, It will be proper here to let them fee (if they be not wilfully ignorant) What it is which makes the Difference of *Baptiſms*: not the *outward Matter* in which they are adminiſtred (for that may be the fame in many *Baptiſms*, as is fhewn.) But *Baptiſms* do differ, 1. In their *Authors.* 2. In the different *Form*, in which they are adminiſtred. 3. In the different *Ends* for which they were inftituted.

And in all thefe the *Baptiſm* of *Chriſt* does differ vaftly from the *Baptiſms* both of *John* and the *Jews*, 1. As to the *Author*: The *Baptiſm* of the *Jews* was an Addition of their own to the Law; and had no higher *Author* that we know of. But *John* was fent by *God*, to *baptize*, John i. 33. And it was *Chriſt the Lord* who was the *Author* of the *Chriſtian Baptiſm.* 2. As to the *Form*: Perfons were *baptized* unto thofe whofe *Difciples* they were admitted by their *Baptiſm.* Thus the *Profelites* to the *Jewiſh Religion*, were *baptized* unto *Mofes.* And Men were made *Difciples* to *John*, by his *Baptiſm.* But the *Chriſtian Baptiſm* alone is adminiſtred *in the name of the Father, and of the Son, and of the Holy Ghoſt.* This is the *Form* of the *Chriſtian Baptiſm*, and which does diftinguifh it from all other *Baptiſms* whatever. 3. The *End* of the *Chriſtian Baptiſm* is as highly diftant and *different* from the *Ends* of other *Baptiſms*, as their *Authors* differ. The *End* of the *Jewiſh Baptiſm* was to give the *Baptized* a Title to the *Priviledges* of the Law of *Mofes.* And the *End* of *John*'s *Baptiſm* was to point to Him who was to come; and to prepare Men, by *Repentance*, for the Reception of the *Gofpel.*

ſpel. But the *End* of Christ's *Baptiſm* was to Inſtate Us into all the Unconceivable *Glories,* and High Eternal *Prerogatives* which belong to the *Members of his Body, of his Fleſh, and of his Bones,* Eph. v. 30. *That we might receive the Adoption of Sons,* Gal. iv. 5. Henceforth no more *Servants,* but *Sons* of God! and *Heirs* of *Heaven!* Theſe are *Ends* ſo far tranſcendent above the *Ends* of all former *Baptiſms;* that, in comparison, other *Baptiſms* are not only *leſs,* but *none at all;* like the Glory of the *Stars,* in preſence of the *Sun ;* they not only are a *leſſer* Light, but when he appears, they become altogether *inviſible.*

And as a *Pledge* or *Fore-taſte* of theſe *Future* and *Boundleſs Joys,* The Gift of the *Holy Ghoſt* is given upon *Earth ;* and is promis'd as an *Effect* of the *Baptiſm* of *Chriſt.* As *Peter* preach- ed, *Acts* ii. 38. *Repent and be baptized every one of you, in the name of Jeſus Chriſt, for the remiſſion of ſins, and ye ſhall receive the gift of the Holy Ghoſt.* And *Gal.* iii. 27. *As many of you as have been baptized into Chriſt, have put on Chriſt.*

This of the *Gift* of the *Holy Ghoſt* was not added to any *Ba- ptiſm* before *Chriſt's :* and does remarkably diſtinguiſh it from all others.

SECT. VI.

That Chriſt *and the* Apoſtles *did not* Baptize *with* John's *Baptiſm.*

THis is a Pretence of the *Quakers* when they find themſelves diſtreſſed with the clear Proofs of *Chriſt* and the *Apoſtles* having adminiſtred *Water-baptiſm.* They ſay that this was *John's* Baptiſm, becauſe it was *Water-baptiſm.* And, as before obſerv'd *Sect.* IV. they only *ſay* this, but can bring no *Proof.* But they put us here again, upon the *Negative,* to prove it was not.

As to their Pretence that it was *John's Baptiſm,* becauſe it was *Water-baptiſm,* that is anſwered in the laſt *Section.*

And now to gratifie them in this (though unreaſonable) De- mand, I will give theſe following Reaſons why the *Baptiſm* which

which *Christ* and his *Apostles* did practise, was not *John's* Baptism:

1st, If *Christ* did *baptize*, with *John's Baptism*; then he made *Disciples* to *John*, and not to himself. For it is before shewn Sect. III. Num. ii & iii. That *Baptism* was an *Initiating Form*, and nothing else, whereby Men were admitted to be *Disciples* to him unto whom they were *baptized*. Thus the *Jews* who were *baptized* unto *Moses* said, *We are Moses's Disciples*. John ix. 28. And those whom *John* baptized, were called the *Disciples* of *John*. And there needs no more to shew that *Christ* did not *baptize* with the *Baptism* of *John*, than to shew that the *Disciples* of *Christ* and of *John* were not the same, which is made evident from *John* i. 35, 37. where it is told that *two* of *John's Disciples* left him, and followed *Jesus*. And *Matth.* xi. 2. *John* sent *two* of his *Disciples* to *Jesus*. And the *Disciples* of *Christ* lived under a different *Oeconomy*, and other *Rules* than either the *Disciples* of *John*, or of the *Pharisees*, to shew that they were under another *Master*. And the *Disciples* of *John* were scandaliz'd at it, *Matth.* ix. 14. *Then came to him* (JESUS) *the Disciples of John, saying, Why do we, and the Pharisees fast oft, but thy Disciples fast not?*

Therefore the *Disciples* of *Christ* and of *John* were not the same: and therefore *Christ* did *baptize* Men to be *his own* Disciples, and not to be the *Disciples* of *John*: and therefore the *Baptism* of *Christ* was not the *Baptism* of *John*.

2dly, If *Christ* did *baptize* with *John's Baptism*, the *more* he *baptized*, it was the more to the *Honour* and *Reputation* of the *Baptism* of *John*: But *Christ's* baptizing was urg'd, by the *Disciples* of *John*, as a lessning of *John*, John iii. 26. Therefore the *Baptism* with which *Christ* did *baptize* cou'd not be the *Baptism* of *John*. Though it be said *John* iv. 2. That *Jesus himself baptized not, but his Disciples*: (For so the *Apostles* and other *Ministers* of *Christ* have *baptized* more into the *Faith* of *Christ*, than *Christ* himself has done:) Yet here is no ground of *Jealousie* or *Rivalship* to *Christ*, because the Administration of *Christ's Baptism*, is all to the *Honour* and *Glory* of *Christ*: And therefore *Christ's* baptizing *more* Disciples than *John*, cou'd be no *Lessning* of *John*, but rather a *Magnifying* of him so much the more, if *Christ* had *baptized* with *John's* Baptism.

3dly,

3dly, When *John's Difciples* had told him of *Chrift's* out ri-
valling him, by *baptizing* more than he, *John* anfwer'd, *He muft
increafe, but I muft decreafe,* John iii. 30. But if CHRIST did *baptize* with the *Baptifm* of *John,* than *John* ftill *increafed,* and
CHRIST *decreafed.* For,

4thly, He is *greater* who *inftitutes* a *Baptifm,* than thofe who
only *adminifter* a *Baptifm* of another's appointment: Therefore
if *Chrift* did *baptize* with the *Baptifm* of *John,* it argues *John* to
be *greater* than *Chrift,* and *Chrift* to be but a *Minifter* of *John.*

5thly, All the *Jews* who had been *baptized* with the *Baptifm*
of *John,* did not turn *Chriftians*; therefore *John's Baptifm* was
not the *Chriftian Baptifm.*

6thly, Thofe of *John's* Difciples, who turned *Chriftians,* were
baptized over again, in the Name of *Chrift*; of which there is a
remarkable Inftance, *Acts* xix. to *v.* 7. But the *fame Baptifm*
was never *repeated* (as is fhewn above, *Sect.* III. *Numb.* iii.)
therefore the *Baptifm* which the *Apoftles* did *adminifter,* was not
John's Baptifm.

7thly, The *Form* of the *Baptifm* which *Chrift* commanded
Mat. xxviii. 19. was, *In the Name of the Father, and of the Son, and
of the Holy Ghoft*: But that was not the *Form* of *John's Baptifm* :
Therefore that was not *John's Baptifm.* See what is before faid
Sect. V. *Num.* ii. of the Difference of *Baptifms,* as to the *Author,*
the *Form,* and the *End* of *each Baptifm*: And, in all thefe Re-
fpects, it is made apparent that the *Baptifm* which was practis'd by *Chrift* and the *Apoftles,* was not the *Baptifm* of *John.*

To all thefe clear Arguments the *Quakers,* without anfwering to any of them, do ftill infift, That the *Water-baptifm*
which the *Apoftles* did adminifter, was no other than *John's* Baptifm. That they had no Command for it ; only did it in Compliance with the *Jews,* as *Paul* circumcis'd *Timothy,* (*Acts* xvi.
3.) And purify'd himfelf in the *Temple,* (*Acts* xxi. 21, *to* 27.)
But this is all *Gratis Dictum* ; here is not one word of *Proof:*
And they might as well fay, That the *Apoftles* PREACHING was
only in Compliance with the *Jews,* and that it was the fame with
John's PREACHING ; for their Commiffions to *Teach,* and to *Baptize* were both given in the fame Breath, *Matth.* xxviii. 19. Go
ye — TEACH *all Nations,* BAPTIZING *them,* &c.

Now why the *Teaching* here fhou'd be *Chrift's,* and *Baptizing*
only

only *John*'s, the *Quakers* are defir'd to give fome other Reafon befides their own *Arbitrary* Interpretations; before which no Text in the *Bible*, or any other Writing can ftand.

Befides, I wou'd inform them, That the *Greek* word μαθητευσατε, in this Text, which we Tranflate *Teach*, fignifies to *make Difciples*; fo that the *literal*, and more *proper* reading of that Text is, *Go, and Difciple all Nations*, or *make Difciples* of them, *baptizing them*, &c.

If it be ask'd, Why we fhou'd Tranflate the Word μαθητευσατε, *Matt*. xxviii. 19. by the Word *Teach*, if it means to *Difciple* a Man, or make him a *Difciple?*

I Anfwer: That *Teaching* was the Method whereby to *Perfwade* a Man, to *Convert* him, fo as to make a *Difciple* of him. But the *Form* of *Admitting* him into the *Church*, and actually to make him a *Difciple*, to give him the *Priviledges* and *Benefits* of a *Difciple*, was by *Baptifm*.

Now the *Apoftles* being fent to *Teach* Men, in order to make them *Difciples*; therefore inftead of Go, *Difciple* Men, we Tranflate it, Go, *Teach*, as being a more Familiar Word, and better underftood in *Englifh*.

Tho' if both the *Greek* words μαθητευσατε, and Βαπτιζοντες, in this Text, were Tranflated Literally, it would obviate thefe *Quaker*-Objections more plainly: For then the Words wou'd run thus; *Go and Admit all Nations to be my Difciples, by Wafhing them with Water, in the Name of the Father, and of the Son, and of the Holy Ghoft*. Διδασκοντες, *Teaching them to obferve all things whatfoever I have commanded you*.

Here the Word Διδασκοντες, i. e. *Teaching*, is plainly diftinguifhed from μαθητευσατε, to *Difciple* them; tho' our *Englifh* renders them both by the Word *Teaching*, and makes a Tautology: *Go Teach all Nations —— Teaching them*.

But, as a *Child* is *Admitted* into a *School* before it be *Taught*: So *Children* may be *Admitted* into the *Pale* of the *Church*, and be made *Difciples*, by *Baptifm*, before they are *Taught*. Which fhews the meaning of thefe two Words, i. e. *Difcipling*, and *Teaching*, to be different. Becaufe, tho' in Perfons Adult, *Teaching* muft go before *Difcipling*; yet in *Children* (who are within the *Covenant*, as of the *Law*, to be Admitted at *eight Days* old, by *Circumcifion*; fo under the *Gofpel*, by *Baptifm*) *Difcipling*

goes

goes before *Teaching :* And that *Difcipling* is only by *Ba-ptifm.*

But to return. The *Quakers* are fo hard put to it, when they are prefs'd with that Text, *Acts* x. 47. *Can any forbid Water,* &c ? That they are forced to make a *Suppofe,* (without any ground or appearance of Truth) That thefe Words were an Anfwer to a Queftion. And that the Queftion was, Whether they might not be Baptized with *John's* Baptifm ? And that this proceeded from a Fondnefs the *Jews* had to *John's* Baptifm. And that the Apoftle *Peter* only Comply'd with them out of Condefcention, as *Paul* Circumcis'd *Timothy.*

Anf. 1. *Cornelius,* and thofe whom *Peter* Baptized, *Acts* x. were *Gentiles* and not *Jews :* They were *Romans,* and therefore cannot be fuppofed to have had any Longing after *John's* Baptifm ; none of them having ever own'd it, or having been Baptiz'd with it.

2. The *Gentile Converts* to *Chriftianity,* refus'd to fubmit to the *Jewifh Circumcifion,* or any of their *Law* (*Acts* xv.) And therefore it is not to be imagin'd, that they wou'd be fond of any of the *Baptifms* which were us'd among the *Jews.*

3. Even all the *Jews* themfelves, no not the *Chief* and *Principal* of them, neither the *Pharifees* nor *Lawyers* did fubmit to *John's* Baptifm, *Luke* vii. 30.

4. The *Ethiopian Eunuch* requefted *Baptifm* from *Philip,* (*Acts* viii.) And it cannot be fuppos'd, that the *Ethiopians* had more knowledge of *John's Baptifm,* or regard for it, than the *Romans,* or great part of the *Jews* themfelves.

5. There is no ground to fuppofe that St. *Peter's* words, *Can any Man forbid Water,* &c ? were an Anfwer to any Queftion that was asked him. The moft forcible *Affirmation* being often exprefs'd by way of *Queftion.*

Can any Man forbid Water ? That is, *No Man can forbid it.* And for the faying, *Then Anfwered Peter.* There is nothing more familiar in the *New Teftament,* than that Expreffion when no *Queftion* at all was asked. See *Matt.* xi. 25. xii. 38. xvii. 4. xxii. 1. *Mark* xi. 14. xii. 35. xiv. 48. *Luke* vii. 40. xiv. 3, 4, 5. xxii. 51. *John* v. 17, 19.

6. Grant-

6. Granting a Queſtion was ask'd, and that *Cornelius*, as well as the *Ethiopian*, had deſir'd *Baptiſm*, why muſt this be conſtru'd of *John's* Baptiſm? Eſpecially conſidering, that *Peter*, in that ſame Sermon which Converted *Cornelius* (Act. x. 37.) told them that the *Goſpel* which he Preached unto them, was that which was *publiſhed, after the Baptiſm which* John *Preached.* What Argument was this for *Cornelius* to return back again to *John's Baptiſm?* Or, if he had deſir'd it, why ſhou'd we think that *Peter* wou'd have *Comply'd* with him; and not rather have *re-prov'd* him, and carry'd him beyond it, to the *Baptiſm* of *Chriſt*: as *Paul* did (*Acts* xix.) to thoſe who had before receiv'd the *Baptiſm* of *John?*

7. But as to the *Complyance* which the *Quakers* wou'd have to *John's Baptiſm*; and which they compare to *Paul's* Complyance in *Circumciſing* Timothy: I will ſhew the great Diſparity.

Firſt, The *Law* was more univerſally receiv'd than *John's Baptiſm*: For *many* and the *Chief* of the *Jews* did not receive *John's Baptiſm*, as above-obſerv'd.

Secondly, The Law was of much longer ſtanding: *John's Baptiſm* was like a *Flaſh* of *Lightning*, like the *Day-Star*, which uſher'd in the *Sun* of *Righteouſneſs*, and then diſappear'd: But the *Law* continu'd during the long *Night* of *Types* and *Shadows*, many *hundreds* of *Years*.

Thirdly, *John* did no *Miracle* (*John* x. 41.) But the *Law* was delivered, and propagated by many *Ages* of *Miracles*. 'Twas enjoyn'd under Penalty of *Death*, to them and their *Poſterities*; whereas *John's Baptiſm* laſted not one Age, was intended only for the Men then preſent, to point out to them the *Meſſiah*, then already come, and ready to appear: And no outward *Penalties* were annexed to *John's Law*; People were only *Invited*, not *Compell'd* to come unto his *Baptiſm*: But to neglect *Circumciſion*, was *Death*, Gen. xvii. 14. Exod. iv. 24.

The *Preaching* of *John* was only a *Warning*; let thoſe take notice to it that wou'd:

Whereas the *Law* was pronounced by the Mouth of *God* Himſelf, in *Thunder* and *Lightning*, and out of the midſt of the *Fire*, upon Mount *Sinai*, in the *Audience* of all the People: *And ſo terrible was the Sight, that* Moſes *ſaid, I exceedingly fear*

D 2

and.

and quake, Heb. xii. 21. For *from God's Right Hand went a Fire of Law for them*, Deut. xxxiii. 2.

From all thefe Reafons, we muſt ſuppoſe the *Jews* to be much more Tenacious of the *Law*, than of *John's Baptiſm* ; and to be brought off with greater difficulty from their *Circumciſion*; which had defcended down to them all the way from *Abraham*; 430 Years before the *Law*, (Gal. iii. 17.) than from *John's Baptiſm*, which was but of Yeſterday ; and never receiv'd by the Chief of the *Jews*. And therefore there was much more reafon for *Paul's* Complying with the *Jews* in the Cafe of *Circumciſion*, than in that of *John's Baptiſm*, as the *Quakers* ſuppoſe.

When *Chriſt* came to fulfil the *Law*, he did it with all regard to the *Law*, (Matth. v. 17, 18; 19.) He *deſtroy'd* it not with *Violence*, all at once ; but *fulfill'd* it *leaſurely* and by *degrees*: *Ut cum honore Mater Synagoga ſepeliretur*. The *Synagogue* was the *Mother* of the *Church* ; and therefore it was fitting that ſhe ſhou'd be *Bury'd* with all *Decency* and *Honour*.

This was the Reafon of all thoſe *Complyances* with the *Jews*, at the *beginning*, to wear them off, by degrees, from their *Superſtition* to the *Law*.

Tho' in this ſome might Comply too far : And there want not thoſe who think that, *Paul's* Circumciſing of *Timothy*, (Acts xvi. 3.) was as *faulty* a *Complyance*, as that which he blam'd in *Peter*, (Gal. ii.) For that of *Paul's* is not Commended, in the Place where it is mentioned.

And now I appeal to the Reafon of Mankind, whether Objections thus pick'd up from ſuch *obſcure* and *uncertain* Paſſages, ought to overballance *plain* and *poſitive Commands*, which are both back'd and explain'd by the *Praëtiſe* of the *Apoſtles*, and the *Univerſal Church* after them ? All which I have before Demonſtrated of *Baptiſm*.

8. But however the *Quakers* may argue from *Paul's* Complyance with the *Jews*, the *Reader* has reafon to complain of my *Complyance* with *Them* : For, after all that has been ſaid, there is not one ſingle Word in any Text of the *N. T.* that does ſo much as hint at any ſuch thing, as that *Peter's* Baptizing of *Cornelius*, or *Philip's* Baptizing of the *Eunuch*, was in any ſort of *Complyance* unto *John's Baptiſm*. This is a perfeët Figment, out of the *Quaker's* own Brain, without any Ground or Foundation

in

in the World : And therefore there was no need of Anſwering it at all, otherwiſe than to bid the *Quakers* prove their *Aſſertion*, That theſe *Baptiſms* were in Complyance with *John*'s, which they cou'd never have done.

Whereas it is plain from the Words of the Text, *(Acts* xvi. 3.) that *Paul*'s Circumciſing *Timothy*, was in Complyance with the *Jews* : It is expreſly ſo ſaid, and the Reaſon of it given, becauſe, tho' his *Mother* was a *Jeweſs*, yet his *Father* was a *Greek* ; and therefore, *becauſe of the* Jews *which were in thoſe Quarters* (ſays the Text) he Circumciſed *Timothy*, that theſe *Jews* might *Hear* and *Receive* him; which, otherwiſe, they wou'd not have done. Now let the *Quakers* ſhew the like Authority, that the *Baptiſms* of *Cornelius*, of the *Eunuch*, and of the *Corinthians*, Acts xviii. 8. (For that too they acknowledge to have been *Water-Baptiſm*, as I will ſhew preſently) let the *Quakers* ſhew the like Authority, as I have given for the *Circumciſion* of *Timothy* being in *Complyance* with the *Jews*; let them ſhew the like; I ſay, that the foreſaid *Baptiſms* were in *Complyance* with *John*'s, and then they will have ſomething to ſay. But till then, this *Excuſe*, or *Put-off* of theirs, is nothing elſe but a *hopeleſs Shift* of a *deſperate Cauſe*, to ſuppoſe, againſt all ſenſe, that theſe *Gentiles*; *(Romans, Ethiopians*, and *Corinthians)* deſir'd *John*'s *Baptiſm*, who rejected all the *Laws* and *Cuſtoms* of the *Jews*.

S E C T. VII.

The Quakers *Maſter-Objection from* 1 Cor. i. 14. *I thank* GOD *that I Baptized none of you, but* Criſpus *and* Gaius. *And* Ver. 17. *For Chriſt ſent me not to Baptize, but to Preach the Goſpel.*

FROM this Paſſage they argue, That *Water-Baptiſm* was not commanded by *Chriſt*, becauſe here St. *Paul* ſays, That he was not ſent to *Baptize* ; and that he thanks God, that he *Baptiz'd* ſo few of them. But,

In

In Anfwer to this, I will firft of all premife, That a bare *Objection*, without fome *Proof* on the other fide, does neither juftifie *their* Caufe, nor overthrow *ours :* For when a thing is Proved *Affirmatively*, it cannot be overthrown by *Negative* Difficulties which may be Objected.

You muft diffolve the *Proofs* which are brought to fupport it : Nothing elfe will do.

For what *Truth* is there fo evident in the World, againft which no Objection can be rais'd ?

Even the Being of a *God* has been difputed againft by thefe fort of Arguments ; that is, by raifing *Objections*, and ftarting *Difficulties*, which may not eafily be Anfwer'd : But while thofe Demonftrative Arguments, which *Prove* a *God*, remain unfhaken, a thoufand *Difficulties* are no *Difproof*.

And fo, while the *Command* of *Chrift*, and the *Practife* of his *Apoftles*, and of all the *Chriftian World*, in purfuance of that Command, are clearly *Prov'd*, no *Difficulty* from an obfcure Text, can fhake fuch a Foundation.

But I lay down this, only as a General Rule ; becaufe this Method is fo much made ufe of by the *Quakers* (and others) who never think of Anfwering plain *Proofs* ; but by raifing a great *Duft* of *Objections*, wou'd *bury* and *hide* what they cannot *Difprove*.

I fay, that I only mind them at prefent, of this fallacious Artifice ; for I have no ufe for it as to thefe *Texts* objected, to which a very plain and eafie Anfwer can be given.   And,

Firft, I would obferve, how the *Quakers* can underftand the Word *Baptize* to mean *Water-Baptifm*, or *no Water-Baptifm*, juft as the *Texts* feem to favour their caufe, or otherwife.

For there is no mention of *Water* in either of the *Texts* objected, only the fingle word *Baptize*.   And why then muft they conftrue thefe *two* Texts only, of all the reft in the *New Teftament*, to mean *Water-Baptifm* ? Why ? but only to ftrain an Objection out of them againft *Water-Baptifm* ?

But will they let the Word *Baptize* fignifie *Water-Baptifm*, in other places, as well as in thefe ?

They

They cannot refuse it with any shew or colour of Reason. They must not refuse it in *Acts* xviii. 8. where the *Baptizing* of *Crispus* (mention'd in the first of the *Texts* objected) is recorded. And there, it is not only said of *Crispus*, that he was *baptized*; but that *many of the* Corinthians *hearing, believed, and were baptized.* By which, the *Quakers* cannot deny *Water-Baptism* to be meant, since they construe it so, 1 *Cor.* i. 14.

Secondly, We may further observe, that in the Text, *Acts* xviii. 8. *Crispus* is only said to have *believed*, which was thought sufficient to infer, that he was *baptized*; which cou'd not be, unless all that *believed*, were *baptized*: Which, no doubt, was the Case, as it is written, *Acts* xiii. 48. *As many as were ordained to eternal Life, believed.* And (Ch. ii. 41.) *They that received the Word, were baptized*, And (V. 47.) *The Lord added to the Church daily such as shou'd be saved.*

So that this is the *Climax* or *Scale* of *Religion*: As many as are ordained to eternal Life do *believe*: And they that *believe*, are *baptized*: And they that are *baptized*, are added to the Church.

And to shew this received Notion, That whoever did *believe* was *baptized*, when *Paul* met some *Disciples* who had not heard of the *Holy Ghost*, *Acts* xix. 3. he did not ask them whether they had been *baptized*, or not? He took that for granted, since they *believed*. But he asks, *Unto what were ye baptized?* Supposing that they had been *baptized*.

Thirdly, Here then this *Objection* of the *Quakers*, has turn'd into an invincible *Argument* against them.

They have, by this, yielded the whole Cause: For if the *Baptism*, 1 Cor. i. 14. be *Water-Baptism*, then that *Baptism*, *Acts* xviii. 8. must be the same: And consequently all the other *Baptisms*, mention'd in the *Acts*, are, as these, *Water-Baptisms* also.

But, besides the *Quakers* Confession (for they are unconstant, and may change their Minds) the thing shews it self, that the *Baptism* mention'd, 1 *Cor.* i. 14. was *Water-Baptism*; because *Paul* there *thanks God, that he baptized none of them but* Crispus *and* Gaius. Wou'd the *Apostle* thank God that he had baptized

so

Fourthly, But now, what is the Reason, that he was glad he had *baptized so few* with *Water-Baptism*? And he gives the Reason, in the very next words. (V. 15.) *Lest any shou'd say, that I had baptized in mine own Name.* What was the occasion of this Fear? It is told from *V.* 10. That there were great *Divisions* and *Contentions* among these *Corinthians*, and that these were grounded upon the Æmulation that arose among them, in behalf of their several *Teachers*. One was for *Paul*, another for *Apollos*, others for *Cephas*, and others for *Christ*.

This wou'd seem, as if the Christian Religion had been contradictory to it self:

As if *Christ*, and *Cephas*, and *Paul*, and *Apollos* had set up against one another:

As if they had not all taught the same Doctrine:

As if each had preach'd up *himself*, and not *Christ*:

And had *baptized* Disciples, each in *his own Name*, and not in *Christ's*; and had begot Followers to *himself*, and not to *Christ*.

To remove this so horrible a Scandal, St. *Paul* argues with great zeal, (V. 13.) *Is Christ divided?* (says he) *Was* Paul *Crucified for you? Or were ye baptized in the Name of* Paul? *I thank God, that I baptized none of you but* Crispus *and* Gaius; *left any should say, That I had baptiz'd in mine own Name*.

There needs no Application of this, the Words of the *Apostle* are themselves so plain.

He did not thank God, that they had not been *baptized*; but that *He* had not done it.

And this, not for any flight to *Water-Baptism*; but to obviate the Objection of his *baptizing* in *his own Name*.

Fifthly, By the way, this is a strong Argument for *Water-Baptism*: Because the *Inward Baptism* of the *Spirit*, cometh not with *Observation* and *Shew*, but is *within* us, *Luk*. xvii. 20, 21. Nor is it done in any Body's *Name*, it is an *inward* Operation upon the *Heart*.

But

·· But the *outward Baptifm* is always · done in fome *Name*
or· other ; in his, *Name* whofe *Difciple* ·you are *thereby* made
and *Admitted.*

Therefore it muft, of neceffity, be the *outward Baptifm*, of
which St. *Paul* here fpeaks ; becaufe it was *outwardly* Adminiftred, in fuch an *outward Name.*.. And he makes this an Argument that he had not made *Difciples* to *himfelf*, but to *Chrift* ;
becaufe he did not *Baptize* them in *his own Name*, but in.
Chrift's.

Now this had been no *Argument*, but perfect *Banter*, if there
had been no *outward Baptifm*, that the People cou'd have both
feen and *heard.* How otherwife cou'd they tell in what *Name*,
or *no Name* they were *baptized*, if all was *Inward* and *Invi-
fible ?*

But I need not prove what the *Quakers* grant and contend for,
that all this was meant of *Water-Baptifm* ;. becaufe otherwife
their whole Objection, from this place, does fall.

VI. But they wou'd infer as if no great ftrefs were laid
upon it ; becaufe that *few* were fo *baptized.*

I Anfwer: That there is nothing in the *Text* which does in-
·fer, that *few* of thefe *Corinthians* were *baptized.*

St. *Paul* only thanks God, that he *himfelf* had not done it,
except to a *few*, for the Reafons before given: But *Acts* xviii. 8.
it is faid, That befides *Crifpus*, whom *Paul* himfelf, *baptized,*
MANY *of the* Corinthians *were baptized.*

Nay, they were all *baptized*, as many as *believed*, as before
is prov'd. And, in this very place, St. *Paul* taking it for granted, that all who *believed*, were *baptiz'd*, which I have already
obferv'd from his Queftion to *certain Difciples*, Acts xix. 3. not
whether they were *baptized*, but *unto what*, i. e. *In what Name*,
they had been *baptized ?* So here 1 *Cor.* i. 13. He does not make
the Queftion, whether they had been *baptized ?* That he takes
for granted. But *in what Name, were ye baptized ?* Which fuppofes, not only that *all* were *baptized*, but likewife that all who
were *baptized*, were baptized in fome *outward Name* ; and therefore that it was the *Outward*, i. e. *Water-Baptifm.* ·· ··

E   VII.

VII. But the second Text objected, *V.* 17. is yet to be accounted for; where St. *Paul* says, *Christ sent me not to Baptize, but to Preach the Gospel.* This he said in justification of himself for having *baptiz'd* so few in that place; for which he blesses God, because, as it happened, it prov'd a great justification of his not baptizing in *his own Name.*

But then, on the other hand, here wou'd seem to be a Neglect in him of his Duty: For if it was his Duty to have baptiz'd them *all*, and he baptiz'd but a *few*, here was a great Neglect.

In Answer to this, we find, that there was no Neglect in not *baptizing* them, for that, not a *few* but *many* of the *Corinthians* were *baptized*, *Acts* xviii. 8. that is, as many as *believed*, as before is shewn.

But then who was it that *baptized* those *many* ? For St. *Paul* baptized but a *few.*

I Answer. The *Apostle* employ'd others, under him, to Baptize.

And he vindicates this, by saying, That he was *not sent to Baptize*, i. e. *principally* and *chiefly*; that was not the *chief* part of his Commission: But the *greater* and more *difficult* part was that of *Preaching*, to *Dispute* with, *Perswade* and *Convert* the *Heathen* World. To this, *great Parts*, and *Courage*, and *Miraculous Gifts* were necessary : But to Administer the *outward Form* of *Baptism* to those who were *Converted*, had no Difficulty in it ; requir'd no great *Parts*, or *Endowments*, only a *lawful Commission* to Execute it.

And it wou'd have taken up too much of the *Apostles* time, it was impossible for them to have *baptized*, with their own Hands, those vast Multitudes whom they Converted. *Christianity* had reach'd to all Quarters of the then known World, as far almost, as at this Day, before the *Apostles* left the World. And cou'd Twelve Men Baptize the *whole World?* Their *Progress* was not the least of their *Miracles :* The *Bread of Life* multiply'd faster, in their *Distribution* of it, than the *Loaves* by our SAVIOUR's *Breaking* of them. St. *Peter* Converted about *three Thousand* at one Sermon, *Acts* ii. 41. And at another time about *five Thousand*, Ch. iv. 4. *Multitudes both of Men and Women.* Ch. v. 14. Many more than the *Apostles* cou'd have *counted*; much more that

than they cou'd have *baptized* ; for which if they had ftay'd,
they had made flender Progrefs. No. The *Apoftles* were fent,
as *loud Heraulds*, to *proclaim* to all the Earth, to run fwiftly, and
gather much People ; and not to ftay (they cou'd not ftay) for
the *baptizing* with their own Hands, all that they Converted :
They left that to others, whom they had ordain'd to Adminifter
it. Yet not fo, as to exclude themfelves ; but they themfelves
did *Baptize*, where they faw occafion, as St. *Paul* here did
Baptize *Crifpus* and *Gaius*, and the Houfe of *Stephanas*, fome
of the Principal of the *Corinthians*. Not that he was oblig'd
to have done it himfelf, having others to whom he might have
left it : For he was not *fent*, that is, put under the *Neceffity* to
Baptize with his own Hands, but to *Preach*, to Convert others,
that was his *principal* Province, and which he was not to neglect, upon the account of *baptizing*, which others could do as
well as he.

But if you will fo underftand the Words of his not being *fent*,
i. e. that it was not within his *Commiffion*, that he was not *Im-
power'd* by *Chrift*, to *Baptize*, then it wou'd have been a *Sin*,
and great *Prefumption* in him, to have *baptized* any body.

Nay more. This Text, thus underftood, is flatly contradictory to *Matt.* xxviii. 19. which fays, Go, *Baptize*: And this
fays, *I am not fent to Baptize*.

Thefe are contradictory, if by, *I am not fent*, be underftood,
I have not *Power* or *Commiffion* to *Baptize*.

But by, *I am not fent*, no more is meant in this *Text*, than
that *Baptizing* is not the *chief* or *principal* part of my *Commiffi-
on*. As if a *General* were accufed for *Muftering* and *Lifting* Men
in his own Name, and not in the *King*'s, and he fhou'd fay, in
Vindication of himfelf, that he had never *lifted* any, except fuch
and fuch *Officers* ; for that he was not *fent* to *Mufter*, or *Drill*
Men, or to Exercife *Troops* or *Regiments*, but to Command the
Army : Wou'd it follow from hence, that he had not Power to
Exercife a *Troop* or a *Regiment*, or that it was not within his
Commiffion ? Or if a *Doctor* of *Phyfick* fhould fay, That it was
not his Part to *compound Medicines*, and make up *Drugs* (that
was the *Apothecary*'s Bufinefs). but to give *Prefcriptions* ; wou'd
any Man infer from this, that he might not *Compound* his own
Medicines if he pleas'd ?

Or

Or if (to come nearer) a *Profeſſor* of *Divinity*, or a *Biſhop* ſhou'd ſay, That he was not *ſent* to *Teach School*; this wou'd not imply that he might not *Keep School*; nay, he ought, if there were no others to do it : So the *Apoſtle* of the *Gentiles* was not *ſent* to ſpend his Time in *Baptizing*, *Viſiting the Sick*, or other Parts of his Duty, (which others might perform) ſo as to hinder his great Work in Converting of the *Gentiles* : All of whom he cou'd not *Baptize*, nor *Viſit* all their *Sick* : Yet both theſe were within his *Commiſſion*, and he *might* and *did* Execute them where he ſaw occaſion. As if all the *Sick* in *London* ſhou'd expect to be *Viſited* by the Biſhop of *London*; and all the *Children* ſhou'd be brought to be *baptized* by him; he might well ſay, That he was not *ſent* to *Baptize*, or to *Viſit* their *Sick*, but to look after his *Epiſcopal* Function : And ſend them for theſe *Offices*, to others, under him : And yet this wou'd no ways imply, that theſe Offices were not within the *Epiſcopal* Commiſſion; or that he was not *ſent* both to *Baptize*, and to *Viſit the Sick* : But only that he was not ſent *principally* and *chiefly* to *Baptize*, or to *Viſit the Sick*.

And as to that Phraſe of being *ſent*; we find it us'd in this ſame ſenſe, to mean only being *chiefly* and *principally* ſent. Thus, *Gen.* xlv. 8. *Joſeph* ſaid to his Brethren, *It was not you that ſent me hither, but God.* It was certainly his *Brethren* who ſent him, for they *ſold* him into *Egypt* : But it was not They, *principally* and *chiefly*, but *God*, who had other and extraordinary Ends in it.

Adam was not deceived (ſays the Apoſtle, 1 *Tim.* ii. 14.) *but the Woman being deceived, was in the Tranſgreſſion.* *Adam* was *deceived*, and *fell* as well as the *Woman*; but the meaning is, he was not *firſt*, or *principally* deceived.

Again. As for you who ſtick ſo cloſe to the *Letter* (when it ſeemeth to ſerve your turn) *Go ye and learn what that meaneth*, I will have Mercy, and not Sacrifice, *Matt.* ix. 13.

By which it cannot be underſtood, that God did not require *Sacrifice*; for he *commanded* it upon Pain of *Death*. Yet he ſays, (Jer. vii. 22.) *I ſpake not unto your Fathers, nor commanded them —— concerning Burnt-Offerings, or Sacrifices : But this thing Commanded I them, ſaying, Obey my Voice*, &c. according as it is written, (1 Sam xv. 22.) *To Obey is better than Sacrifice.*

By

By all which cannot be meant, that God did not Command the *Jews* concerning *Burnt-Offerings* and *Sacrifices* (for we know how particularly they were commanded) but that the *outward Sacrifice* was not the *chief* and *principal* part of the Command; which respected *chiefly* the *inward* Sacrifice and Circumcision of the *Heart*.

Which when they neglected, and lean'd wholly to the *Outward*, then God detests their *Oblations*; Isa. i. 14. *Your new Moons, and your appointed Feasts my Soul hateth, I am weary to bear them.* And he says, V. 12. *Who hath required this at your Hand?*

It was certainly God who had *required* all these things at their hands; but these *outward Performances*, (tho' the *Neglect* or *Abuse* of them was punished with *Death*) yet they were not the *chief* and *principal* part of the Command, being intended *chiefly* for the sake of the *Inward* and *Spiritual* Part : From which when they were separated, they were (like the *Body*, when the *Soul* is gone) a *dead* and a *loathsome*. C ARCASS of *Religion*: And which God is therefore said, not to have commanded, because he did not Command them without the other : As he made not the *Body* without the *Soul* ; yet he made the *Body* as well as the *Soul*.

VIII. And as there is *Soul* and *Body* in *Man*, so (while *Man* is in the *Body*) there must be a *Soul* and *Body* of *Religion* ; that is, an *outward* and an *inward* W O R S H I P, with our *Bodies* as well as our *Souls*.

And as the Separation of *Soul* and *Body* in *Man*, is called *Death* ; so is the Separation of the *outward* and the *inward* Part of *Religion*, the *Death* and *Destruction* of *Religion*.

The *outward* is the *Cask*, and the *inward* is the *Wine*. The *Cask* is no Part of the *Wine* ; but if you break the *Cask*, you lose the *Wine*. And as certainly, whoever destroy the *outward* Institutions of *Religion*, lose the *inward* Parts of it too.

As is sadly experienc'd in the *Quakers*, who, having thrown off the *outward Baptism*, and the other *Sacrament* of *Christ's Death*, have, thereby, lost the *inward* thing signify'd, which is, the P E R S O N A L *Christ*, as Existing *without all other Men*, and having so *Suffer'd*, *Rose*, *Ascended*, and now, and for ever,

Sitteth

Sitteth in *Heaven,* in his true proper *Human Nature,* Without *all other Men.* This the *Quakers* will not own, (except some of the *New* Separation) and this they have lost, by their Neglect of those *outward Sacraments,* which *Christ* appointed for this very End (among others) that is, as *Remembrances* of his *Death :* For it had been morally impossible for Men, who had *constantly* and with *due Reverence,* attended these holy *Sacraments* of *Baptism* and the *Lord's Supper,* ever to have *forgot* his *Death,* so lively represented before their Eyes, and into which they were *baptized ;* or to have turn'd all into a mœer *Allegory,* perform'd *within* every Man's *Breast,* as these *Quakers* have done.

But the *Enemy* has perswaded them to break the *Cask,* and destroy the *Body* of *Religion ;* whereby the *Wine* is spilt, and the *Soul* of *Religion* is fled from them : And by neglecting the *outward Part,* they have lost the whole *inward,* and *Truth* of *Religion ;* which is a true *Faith* in the O u t w a r d *Christ,* and in the *Satisfaction* made for our *Sins,* by his *Blood* O u t w a r d l y *shed ;* and in his *Intercession,* in our *Nature,* as our *High-Priest,* at his *Father's* Right Hand, *now,* in *Heaven ;* into which *Holy of Holies,* He has carry'd his own *Blood* of *Expiation, once* offer'd upon the *Cross,* and *presents* it, for *ever,* as the *Atonement* and full *satisfaction* for the *Sins* of the *whole World ;* but apply'd only by true *Faith* and *Repentance,* thereby, becomes fully Effectual to the *Salvation* of every *Faithful Penitent.*

This is the only true *Christian Faith :* And from this the *Quakers* have totally fallen ; and that chiefly, by their *Mad* throwing off the O u t w a r d *Guards, Preservatives, Fences, Sacraments,* and *Pledges* of *Religion.* And those O u t w a r d *Means of Grace,* which *Christ* has commanded, and given us as the only Outward Grounds for our *Hope of Glory.* For how can that Man get to *Heaven,* who will not go the way that *Christ* has appointed ; who came down from *Heaven,* on purpose to *shew* and *lead* us the way thither ; yet we will be *wiser* than he, find fault with his *Institutions,* as being too much upon the *Outward ;* and think that we can and may *Spiritualize* them *finer,* and make the way *shorter* than he has done

IX.

IX. But to return, if the *Quakers* cou'd find fuch *Texts* concerning *Baptifm*, as I have fhewn above concerning *Sacrifices*, as if it were faid, 'That *God* did *not command* Baptifm ; that he *hated it*, and was *weary to bear it*, that *he would not have it*, &c. If fuch *Texts* cou'd be found, How wou'd the *Quakers* triumph! Who wou'd be able to ftand before them! And yet, if fuch were found, they wou'd prove no more againft the *outward* BAPTISM, than they did againft the *outward* SACRIFICES, *i. e.* That if any regarded nothing elfe in *Baptifm*, than the *outward Wafhing*, it wou'd be as hateful to God, as the *Jewifh Sacrifices*, when they regarded nothing more in them but the *Outward.*

And it may be truly faid, That God did not Command either fuch *Sacrifices*, or fuch a *Baptifm* ; becaufe he commanded not the *outward* alone, but with refpeҫt unto, and *chiefly* for the fake of the *Inward.*

And, therefore, as all thefe, and other the like Expreffions in the *Old Teftament* did not at all tend to the *Abolition*, only to the *Reҫtification* of the Legal *Sacrifices :* So, much lefs, can that fingle Expreffion, 1 *Cor.* i. 17. of *Paul*'s faying (upon the occafion, and in the fenfe above mention'd) that *he was not fent to Baptize, but to Preach*, much lefs can this infer the *Abolition* of *Baptifm* ; being as pofitively *commanded*, as *Sacrifices* were under the *Law*, and as certainly *praҫtis'd* by the *Apoftles*, as the *Sacrifices* were by the *Levitical Priefts.*

X. Now fuppofe that I fhould deny, that OUTWARD *Sacrifices* were ever *commanded* ; or, that the *Jews* did ever *praҫtife* them: And fhou'd Interpret all that is faid of *Sacrifices*, only of the *Inward*, as the *Quakers* do of *Baptifm* ; and I fhou'd produce the *Texts* above quoted to prove that God did not command *Sacrifices*, which are much more pofitive than that *fingle one* which is ftrain'd againft *Baptifm* : I fay, fuppofe that I fhou'd be fo Extravagant as to fet up fuch a Notion, what Method (except that of *Bedlam*, which, in that Cafe, wou'd be moft proper) cou'd be taken to convince me ? And fuppofe I fhou'd gain as many *Profelytes* as G. *Fox* has done: And we fhou'd boaft
our

our *Numbers,* and *Light within,* &c. wou'd not this following Method be taken with us?

1ft. To see how *Sacrifices* are actually us'd *now* in those Parts of the World where they do *Sacrifice.* And being convinc'd that these do use *outward Sacrifices,* and understand the first Command to *Sacrifice,* in that sense, to inquire

2dly, Whether they did not receive this from their *Fathers,* so upward, to the first Institution? And is not this the surest Rule to find out the meaning of the *first Command? viz.* How it was *understood* and *practis'd* by those to whom the Command was *first* given; and from them, through all Ages since. Upon all which *Topicks,* the present *Water-Baptism,* now us'd, may be as much demonstrated to be the same which was *practis'd* by the *Apostles,* and consequently, which was *commanded* by *Christ,* as the *outward Sacrifices* can be shewn to have been, at first, *commanded* to the *Jews,* and *practis'd* by them.

XI. And as for that precarious Plea, before confuted, of the *Baptism* which the *Apostles* practis'd, being only a Complyance with the *Jews*; there is more *Pretence* to say, that the *Jewish Sacrifices* were in Complyance with the *Heathen Sacrifices,* which were long before the *Levitical Law.*

I say, there is more *Pretence* for this, but not more *Truth.* More *pretence,* because it has been advanced of late, by Men of greater Figure than *Quakers,* That the *Levitical Sacrifices* were commanded by God, in Complyance with the *Gentile Sacrifices,* which were before used.

But this is a Subject by it self. I now only shew the *Quakers,* that there is more ground to *spiritualize* away *Sacrifices* from the *Letter,* than *Baptism*; more *pretence* for it from *Texts* of *Scripture,* and from some *odd Opinions* of some Learned Men.

And if the Denial of O u t w a r d *Sacrifices* wou'd be counted (as the like of *Baptism* was, when *first* started) to be nothing short of *Madness,* the continuance of that *Distraction* for 46 Years together (as in the Case of *Baptism*) might make it more *familiar* to us, but would abate nothing of the *Unreasonableness.*

XII.

XII. I believe the Reader, by this time, cannot but think that I have taken too much needlefs Pains, in Anfwer to that Objection of St. *Paul's* faying that he was not fent to *Baptize*, but to *Preach :* But I fpeak to a fort of Men, who are us'd to *Repetitions,* and will not take a *Hint* (unlefs it be on their fide) and therefore I enlarge more than I wou'd do, if I were writing to any others. But I think I have faid enough, even to them, to fhew, that the Meaning of the *Apoftle* in this *Text,* was only to prefer the Office of *Preaching,* before that of *Baptizing.* But I muft withal defire them to take notice, that the *Preaching,* that is, *Publifhing* of the *Gofpel,* at firft to *Heathens,* was a very different thing, and of much greater *Neceffity,* than thofe fet *Difcourfes,* which we now call *Preaching* in *Chriftian* Auditories.

XIII. Let me (to conclude) add one Argument more, from this Text, *1 Cor.* i. 17. why that *Baptifm ;* mention'd *Matt.* xxviii. 19. cannot be meant of the *Baptifm with the Holy Ghoft.* Becaufe if when *Chrift* fent his *Apoftles* to *Baptize,* the meaning was (as the *Quakers* wou'd have it) to *Baptize* with the *Holy Ghoft*; then the Apoftle *Paul* faid in this *Text,* 1 Cor. i. 17. That he was not *fent* to *Baptize* with the *Holy Ghoft.* Which fenfe, fince the *Quakers* will not own, they cannot reconcile thefe *Texts,* without confeffing, that that Text, *Matt.* xxviii. 19. was not meant of the *Baptifm* with the *Holy Ghoft,* and then it muft be meant of the *Water-Baptifm.*

SECT. VIII.

Objection from 1 Pet. iii. 21.

THE Words of the *Text* are thefe. *The like Figure whereunto (i. e.* the *Ark) even Baptifm, doth alfo now fave us, (not the putting away of the Filth of the Flefh, but the Anfwer of a Good Confcience towards God) by the Refurrection of Jefus Chrift.*

F

From

From whence the *Quakers* argue thus: That *Baptism* doth not consist in the *outward Washing*, but the *inward*.

And so far they argue right, That the *inward* is the *chief* and *principal* part; and therefore, that if any regard only the *outward Washing* of the *Skin*, in *Baptism*, they are indeed frustrated of the whole Benefit of it, which is altogether *Spiritual*.

And it has been observ'd *Sect*. VII. latter part of *Numb*. vii. That if only the *outward* Part of the *Sacrifices*, or *Circumcision*, and other *Institutions* under the *Law*, were regarded, they were *hateful* to *God*, and he *rejected* them; tho', at the same time, he commanded the Performance of them, under the Penalty of *Death*.

Thus it is in the *Institutions* of the *Gospel*. The *Inward* and *Spiritual* Part is the *chief*; and for the sake of which only, the *Outward* is commanded: But this makes the *Outward* necessary, instead of throwing it off; because (as it was under the *Law*) the *Outward* was ordained as a *Means* whereby we are made Partakers of the *Inward*: And therefore, if we neglect and despise the *Outward*, when we may have it, we have no Promise in the *Gospel* to Intitle us to the *Inward*: As he that neglects the *Means*, has no Reason to expect the *End*. It is true, a *Miracle* may do it; but it is *Presumption*, and *Tempting* of *God*, to neglect the *Outward Means* of *God's* Appointment, in expectation of his *Miraculous* Interposition, against the *Method* which he has commanded. As if *provoking* of *God*, did Intitle us the more to his *Protection*! Or, as if we were *Wiser* than *He*, to *mend* and *alter* his *Institutions*, and *dispense* with them, at our Pleasure!

Here let it be minded, that the *Ark* is put only as a *Type* of *Baptism*: Therefore *Baptism* is the more *worthy*, and more *necessary*. And to neglect *Baptism*, is to venture *swimming* in the *Deluge*, without the *Ark*.

SECT. IX.

The Quaker-Objection from, Eph. iv. 5.

I. THE Words of the Text are thefe. *One Lord, one Faith, one Baptifm*; whence the *Quakers* argue thus. That *Water-Baptifm* is one *Baptifm*, and the *Baptifm* with the *Holy Ghoft*, is another *Baptifm*; becaufe the *one* is the *Outward*, and the other the *Inward* Baptifm; and *outward* and *inward* are *two* Things: Therefore that thefe muft be *two* Baptifms: which, they fay, is contrary to this *Text*, that fays, the *Chriftians* have but O N E *Baptifm*, as they have but O N E *Lord*, and O N E *Faith*.

II. I Anfwer. *Outward* and *Inward* are *Two* things; but yet they hinder not the *Unity* of *that* which is compos'd of *Both*. Thus *Soul* and *Body* are *Two* things, and of *Natures* the moft different of any Two things in the World; yet they hinder not the *Unity* of the *Man*, who is compos'd of *Both*. Nay, it is the *Compofition* of thefe Two that makes up the *One* M A N; infomuch, that when thefe *Two* are *Divided*, the M A N is no more; for it is nothing elfe which we call *Death*, but the *Separation* of *Soul* and *Body*.

And (as before fhewn, *Sect.* VII. *Num.* VIII.) while there is *Soul* and *Body* in *Man*, there muft be a *Soul* and *Body* of *Religion*, that is, an *Outward* and an *Inward* Part of *Religion*: And if we deftroy the *Outward*, we fhall lofe the *Inward*; becaufe the *Outward* was defign'd for the Safety and Prefervation of the *Inward*.

It is true, that the *Inward* is the *Chief* and *Principal* Part, as of *Man*, fo of his *Religion* : But this does not infer, that the *Outward* is not likewife neceffary. We are commanded, *Rom.* xii. 1. to *Prefent our* Bodies *a living Sacrifice*, and this is call'd our *Reafonable Service*. For, is it not Reafonable, that, fince our *Bodies* are *God's* Creatures, as well as our *Souls*, He fhould have the *Adoration* and *Service* of our *Bodies*, as well as of our *Souls* ?

There

There is no *Outward* or *Publick* WORSHIP but by our *Bodies* ; we cannot *otherwise* expreſs the INWARD *Devotion* and *Adoration* of our *Minds*.

And this is ſo *Natural*, that whoever has a due *Reverence* and *Awe* of the *Divine Majeſty*, cannot help to Expreſs it *Outwardly*, by the *Adoration* of his *Body*, in his Approaches to God, even tho' in *Private*. As our *Bleſſed Saviour*, in His *Agony*, fell *proſtrate* upon *His Face* to the Earth.

And whoever deny the *Outward Worſhip* to God, or perform. it *ſlovenly*, and *careleſly*, it is a full Demonſtration that they have no *True* and *Real Devotion*, or *Juſt Apprehenſion* of the *Almighty*.

Therefore the *Outward* Part of *Religion* muſt, by no means, be let go, becauſe the *Inward* certainly dies, when the *Outward* is gone.

But the *Outward* and the *Inward* WORSHIP of *God* are not *Two* Worſhips, but only Two *Parts* of the *ſame* Worſhip. As *Soul* and *Body* are not *Two Men*, but *Two Parts* of the *ſame* Man ; ſo the Adoration of this *One* Man, *Outwardly* in his *Body*, and *Inwardly* in his *Soul*, is not Two *Worſhips*, but Two *Parts* of the SAME *Worſhip*.

III. There is but *one Faith*, yet this *Faith* conſiſts of *ſeveral Parts*. There is a *Faith* in *God*, of which the *Heathens* do partake: There is a *Faith* in *Chriſt*, which denominates Men *Chriſtians* : Yet theſe are not *Two Faiths* in a *Chriſtian*, but Two *Parts* of the SAME *Faith*. There is likewiſe a *Faith* in the *Promiſes* of the *Goſpel* ; and that what is therein *Commanded*, is from *God* : And there are Degrees of this *Faith*, of which one Chriſtian does partake more than another. And yet to *Chriſtians* there is but *One Faith*.

The Belief of a *God*, and of *Chriſt*, are Two *Faiths* or *Beliefs*, becauſe many do Believe a *God*, who do not Believe in *Chriſt* : Yet, in a *Chriſtian* they are not Two *Faiths*, but ONE *Faith* ; becauſe the *one*, that is, the *Faith* in *Chriſt*, does ſuppoſe the *other*, that is, the *Belief* of a *God* ; it only *Adds* to it, and *Builds* upon it. And this makes them no more Two *Faiths*, than building an Houſe a *Story* higher makes it Two *Houſes*.

IV. There

IV. There is but *One Lord*, that is *Chriſt*; yet He conſiſts of an *Outward* and an *Inward* Part, of *Body* and *Soul*. Nay more, of both the *Divine* and *Human Natures*. I might urge the different *Perſons* in the *One Divine Nature*; but this will be no Argument to the *Quakers*, who Deny it. But they Deny not (ſeemingly at leaſt) the *Divinity* of *Chriſt*; and therefore, as this *Lord* is but *One*, tho' conſiſting of ſeveral *Natures*; and His *Faith* and *Worſhip* but *One*, tho' conſiſting of ſeveral *Parts*; why may not His *Baptiſm* be likewiſe *One*, tho' conſiſting of an *Outward* and an *Inward* Part?

V. There was an *Outward* and an *Inward* CIRCUMCISION, as well as an *Outward* and *Inward* BAPTISM; yet no Man will ſay, that there were T w o *Circumciſions* under the *Law*. As little Reaſon is there to ſay, That there are T w o *Baptiſms* under the *Goſpel*. See what is before ſaid, *Sect*. VII. *Num*. X, & XI, of the ſtronger Preſumptions to deny the *Outward* SACRIFICES under the *Law*, than the *Outward* BAPTISM under the *Goſpel*.

VI. Let me add, that *Circumciſion* was diſcontinu'd 40 Years in the Wilderneſs *(Joſh*. v. 5.) yet this was made no Argument againſt the *Reviving* and *Continuance* of it afterwards.

But *Baptiſm* has not been diſcontinu'd *one Year*, nor at all in the *Chriſtian Church*, ſince its firſt Inſtitution by *Chriſt*.

If the *Quakers* cou'd find ſuch a *Diſcontinuance* of *Baptiſm*, as there was of *Circumciſion*, they wou'd make great Advantage of it; tho' it cou'd be no more an Argument in the one caſe, than in the other.

But ſince they have not even this ſmall Pretence againſt it, the *Conſtant* and *Uninterrupted Practice* of *Baptiſm*, in all *Chriſtian Churches*, through all *Ages*, is an Irrefragable Argument againſt them; and ſhews them to be Diſſonant from the whole Church of CHRIST.

SECT.

SECT. X.

An Objection from Heb. vi. 1.

I. I Cou'd not have imagin'd that this shou'd have been made an *Objection*, if I had not seen it urg'd as such, in a Book printed this Year, 1696. Intituled, *John Baptist's Decreasing*, &c. By *John Gratton*. Where he urges mightily this Text, as a plain Prohibition to the further *Continuance* of *Baptism*. He lays great stress upon the Word *Leaving*. *Therefore Leaving the Principles of the Doctrine of Christ, let us go on unto Perfection*. LEAVING (saith he, P. 45.) *Mark*, LEAVING *the Principles*, &c. And *Baptism* being nam'd in the second Verse, he infers, That the *Apostle* here Commands to *leave off* the Practice of *Baptism*, which, he says, had been Indulg'd to the first *Converts* to *Christianity*, with other *Jewish Ceremonies*. As to the supposed *Indulging* of *Baptism*, on account of its being a *Jewish Ceremony*, it is answer'd before, Sect. VI. Pag. 19, 20, 21. But now as to this Inference from *Heb*. vi. 1. *John Gratton* says, P. 47. That this word LEAVING *seems to entail the foregoing words in the Chapter before, where he* (the Apostle) *had been telling them of their Childishness* (he mentions the Doctrine of *Baptism*, which cannot prove the *Imposing* of Water-Baptism, *any more than all the rest*) *and was now for bringing them on to a further State, where they might know Perfection* —— *And it seems clear to me, that there was some need for those things, they had so long lain like Children weak, and Babes in, to be left*. Therefore leaving these, let us go on to Perfection ; *and saith further ;* This will we do, if God permit : *But if they had been commanded by Christ, to have been used to the World's End, then why shou'd* Paul *have been so earnest at that Day, which was soon after Christ's Ascension, to have had them then to leave them ?* These are his words, and a great deal more to the same purpose. And in the same Page, he ranks *Baptism* with *Circumcision*, *Passover*, and other *Jewish Rites*.

II. But

II. But it is very wonderful, how any Man cou'd shut his Eyes so hard, as to oversee not only the whole *Scope*, but the very *Words* of this *Text*. Can such a Blindness be other than wilful? The *Apostle* was reproving some of the *Hebrews* for their slender Proficiency in the Knowledge of the *Gospel*. And that he cou'd not lead them to the *Higher Mysteries*, they hardly yet being well fixed in the very *Rudiments* and *Fundamentals* of *Christianity*: As if one shou'd say, That he would make an ill *Doctor* of *Divinity*, who had not yet learned his *Catechism*.

For the *Apostle* in the former Chapter having treated of the Mysterious Parallel 'twixt *Christ* and *Melchisedec*, he stops short, Ver. 11, upon the account of their Incapacity, *of whom* (that is, of *Christ* and *Melchisedec*) *we have many things to say, and hard to be uttered, seeing ye are dull of hearing: For when for the time ye ought to be Teachers, ye have need that one teach you again, which be the first Principles of the Oracles of God.* Then he goes on to provoke them to a further *Proficiency* in the words of the Text we are now considering, *Therefore* (says he) *leaving the Principles of the Doctrin of Christ, let us go on unto Perfection, not laying again the Foundation of Repentance from dead Works, and of Faith towards God, of the Doctrin of Baptisms, and of laying on of Hands, and of the Resurrection of the Dead, and of Eternal Judgment. And this will we do, if God permit.*

Here is the Doctrine of *Baptism* placed in the very Heart of the *Fundamentals* of *Christianity*; yet the *Quakers* would filch it out from amongst all the rest, and refer *it alone* to the *Ceremonials* of the Law spoken of in the former Chapter. This was drop'd at a venture; for the *former Chapter* treats only of the *Melchisedecal Priesthood*, which was no Part of the *Law*; and there are none of the *Legal Types* or *Ceremonies* so much as mention'd in it. Yet *Baptism* in the next Chapter must refer to them!

There cannot be a greater *Confession* to *Baptism* than this *Objection* of the *Quakers*; nor a stronger Proof for the *Necessity* of it, than to see it rank'd with these most-acknowledg'd *Foundations* of *Christian* Religion, and call'd one of the *First Principles of the Oracles of God*.

III. And

III. And as to the word *Leaving*, upon which this Author lays fo great a ftrefs, in this *Text*, as if it meant *Forfaking* and *Abandoning*, it is ftrange that he fhould bring in the *Apoftle* Exhorting to *Leave off*, and *Forfake* the *Principles* of the *Doctrine* of *Chrift!* But *Leaving* there is very plainly meant of *leaving* or *intermitting* (as the *Vulgar* renders it) to *treat* further at that time of thefe *Principles*, which the *Apoftle* is fo far from *forfaking*, that he fixes them as the *Foundation*; which he fays he will not *lay again*, as fuppofing it *laid already*; but build further upon it, improve and carry up the *Superftructure*. So that this *Leaving*, is only *leaving* or *ceafing* to *Difcourfe* further upon thefe *Principles, Intermittentes Sermonem, intermitting* or *breaking off* the *Debate*. Which is literally, according to the *Greek* ἀφέντες λόγον, *leaving that Word* or *Subject* of which he then fpoke, he went on to difcourfe of other things.

The Reader could not forgive this Trifling in me, to prove things which are felf-evident, if he did not fee that I am forc'd to it.

However, this Advantage is gain'd by it, to fee the very flender *Foundations* upon which the *Quakers* build their Objections againft *Baptifm*; which they muft either grant to be one of the *Principles* of *Chriftianity*, or that *Faith* and *Repentance* are not.

IV. But indeed (it is frightful to fay it, I pray God they may ferioufly confider of it) they have, together with *Baptifm*, thrown off all the other *Principles* of the *Doctrin* of *Chrift*, which are mention'd in this *Text*. 1. *Repentance*. Againft this they have fet up a *Sinlefs Perfection*, which needeth no *Repentance*. They never beg Pardon for *Sin*, fuppofing they have none; and mock at us for faying, *Lord have Mercy upon us*; and upbraid our *Liturgy* for having a *Confeffion* of *Sin* in it. *Edward Burrough*, p. 32. of his Works, printed 1672, fays, That *God doth not accept of any, where there is any failing, or who doth not fulfill the Law, and doth not Anfwer every Demand of Juftice.* 2. *Faith towards God.*

See The Snake in the Grafs, 1ft *Part*, or *Preface*, p. 313, 314. 2d *Part*, p. 40, 41, 61, 62.

Th is

This is the *Chriſtian* Faith ; or Faith in God through *Chriſt*. But the *Quakers* ſay, That they can come to God *Immediately*, without the *Mediation* of *Chriſt*, and therefore they do not *Pray* to *Chriſt*, whom they *utterly deny* to be that Perſon who ſuffer'd for them upon the Croſs ; as Mr. *Penn* in his *Serious Apology*, p. 146. Part 1.p 330, 331.

They make *Chriſt* to be nothing elſe than what they call *The Light within* ; which, they ſay, is ſufficient of itſelf, without any thing elſe, to bring us to God ; and that whoever follows it, needs no other Help.

Now they ſay, That all the *Heathen*, every Man that is born into the World, has this *Light within*, that is, *Chriſt* ; and, that this *Light within* is ſufficient for his *Salvation*, without any thing elſe : Whereby they take away any Neceſſity of an *Outward Chriſt* to *dye* for our *Sins*, and make the *Heathen* Faith as good as the *Chriſtian* : And therefore they have taken away that *Chriſtian Faith towards God*, which is the Second of the *Principles* mention'd in this *Text*. The Third is *Baptiſm*, which they openly diſclaim. The Fourth is, the *laying on of Hands*, that is, the *Ordination, Confirmation*, and *Abſolution* of the *Church*, which are all perform'd by *laying on of Hands*. And how much ſoever the *Quakers* and others do deſpiſe them, yet the *Apoſtle* here reckons them among the *Fundamentals* : For the *Government* and *Diſcipline* of the *Church* are *Eſſential* to it, as it is a *Society*, it could not otherwiſe be a *Society*. The Sin of *Korah* was nothing but concerning *Church-Government*. And *Aaron*'s *Rod* that Budded, in confirmation of his *Prieſthood*, was ordained to be kept for ever in the Num. 16, & 17 C. *Ark*, for a Token againſt the *Rebels* ; ſo are they call'd, who *Rebel*'d againſt that *Prieſthood* which God had then appointed by *Moſes* ; and the Sin cannot be leſs to *Rebel* againſt that *Prieſthood* which *Chriſt* himſelf appointed. Which is ſhewn more at large in the *Diſcourſe* mention'd in the *Advertiſement*.

Now if *Aaron*'s *Rod*, that is, *Church-Government*, was one of the *Three* ſacred *Depoſitums* which were ordain'd to be kept in the *Ark*, why ſhould we wonder to ſee it here placed among the *Fundamentals* of *Chriſtianity* ?

The *Pot of Manna, Aaron*'s *Rod*, and the *Tables of* Heb. ix. 4. *the Covenant*, were all that was kept in the *Ark*.

Which

Which shews *Church-Government* to be *Necessary* next to our *Manna*, the very Support of our *Life*; and the best Guard to preserve the *Decalogue*, *i. e.* our Duty to *God* and *Man*.

V. And tho' the *Quakers* cry down *Church-Authority* in others, yet they magnifie it as much in themselves as any *Church* whatsoever.

The Ingenious *W. P.* in his *Judas and the Jews*, writing against some *Dissenters* amongst the *Quakers*, asserts the *Authority* of the *Church* very high, and *the Power of the Elders in the Church*, p. 13. and presses that Text, *Matth.* xviii. 17. *Tell it unto the Church*, to extend to Matters of *Faith* and *Worship*, as well as to Private *Injuries* or *Offences* amongst *Christians*. *That Christ* (says he) *as well gave His Church Power to Reject as to Try Spirits, is not hard to prove. That notable Passage,* Go, tell the Church, *does it to our hand : For if in case of private Offence betwixt Brethren, the Church is made Absolute Judge, from whom there is no Appeal in this World; how much more in any the least case that concerns the* NATURE, BEING, FAITH, *and* WORSHIP *of the Church her self?*

But the Case was quite alter'd when he came to Answer that same *Text*, as urged against the *Quakers* by the *Church*; which he does in his *Address to Protestants*, p. 152, 153, & 154. of the *Second Edition* in *Octavo*, printed 1692. And then that Text does not relate at all to *Faith* or *Worship*, but only to *private Injuries*. For having deny'd the *Authority* of the *Church* in Matters of *Faith*, he puts the Objection thus against himself : *But what then can be the meaning of Christ's Words; Go, tell the Church? Very well. I Answer* (says he, *p. 153.*) *'Tis not about* Faith, *but* Injury, *that Christ speaks; and the place explains itself, which is this*; Moreover, if thy Brother shall TRESPASS against THEE, go and tell him his FAULT, between thee and him alone. *Here is* Wrong, *not* Religion; Injustice, *not* Faith *or* Conscience *concern'd; as some would have it, to maintain their Church-Power.* —— *The words* TRESPASS *and* FAULT *prove abundantly, that He only meant* Private *and* Personal Injuries; *and that not only from the common and undeniable signification and use of the words* TRESPASS *and* FAULT, *but from the way Christ directs and commands for Accommodation,* viz. *That the Person wronged speak* to him that commits the Injury, alone; if that will not do, that he take one or two with him: But no man can think, that if it related to FAITH or WORSHIP, I ought to Receive the Judgment of one, or two, or three, for a sufficient Rule.——Therefore it cannot relate to Matters of FAITH, and Scruples of CONSCIENCE, but PERSONAL and PRIVATE INJURIES.

Thus he. But tho' the Judgment of one, two, or three, is not of itself a sufficient Rule, (none ever said it was) yet may not one, two, or three ADMONISH one another, even in Matters of Faith and Worship, as well as of Private Injuries, and, in case of Refractoriness and Obstinacy, bring the Cause before the Church? Thou shalt in any wise Rebuke thy Neighbour, and not suffer Sin upon him. Yet was not the Judgment of every Man a sufficient Rule to his Neighbour. And our Saviour's commanding to bring the Cause finally before the Church, shews plainly, that the Judgment of the one, two, or three, was not meant for a sufficient Rule, that is, the ultimate Decision.

Lev. xix. 17.

But in Answer to Mr. Penn's Argument, That this Text, Tell it unto the Church, was meant only of Private Injuries, I shall repeat but his own words before quoted, and grant, that as it was meant of Private Injuries, so, as Mr. Penn very well infers, How much more in any the least Case that concerns the Nature, Being, Faith, and Worship of the Church her self?

VI. But, to return. The fifth Article in that Enumeration of Fundamentals, Heb. vi. 1, & 2. is, The Resurrection of the Dead; which the Quakers do likewise deny; as it is fully prov'd in The Snake in the Grass, Par. 2. Sect. 13.

The last is that of Eternal Judgment, which depends upon the former, and may be made one with it; and is likewise deny'd by the Quakers, that is, turn'd into Hymeneus and Philetus's Sense, of an Inward only and Spiritual Resurrection, or Judgment perform'd within us. I have frequently heard Quakers say, that they expected no other Resurrection or future Judgment, than what they had attain'd already, that is, the Resurrection of Christ, or the Light; and the Judgment or Condemnation of Sin, in their Hearts.

George

George Whitehead, in his Book call'd *The Nature of Chriſtia-*
nity, &c. printed 1671, p. 29, thus ridicules it: *Doſt thou* (ſays
he to his Opponent) *look for Chriſt, as the Son of* Mary, *to Ap-*
pear outwardly, in a Bodily Exiſtence, to ſave thee? If thou doſt,
thou mayſt look until thy Eyes drop out, before thou wilt ſee ſuch
an Appearance of him.

And now what Wonder is it, that theſe ſhould throw off
Baptiſm, who have likewiſe thrown off all the other *Funda-*
mentals, which are reckon'd with it in this *Text?*

VII. But let us hence obſerve, and beware of *Neglecting* or
Deſpiſing the *Outward* Inſtitutions of *God*; becauſe theſe de-
pending upon the Authority of *God*, no leſs than the *Inward*
and *Spiritual*, rejecting of the one overthrows the *Obligation*
and *Sanction* of the whole, and is a rejecting of *God* the
Inſtitutor; who, in His juſt Judgment, ſuffers thoſe to loſe
the one, that think themſelves too good for the other.

Men were made Partakers of Chriſt *to come*, by the *Sa-*
crifices which were appointed, as *Types* of Him, under the
Law: So now are we Partakers of Him, *who is come*, by the
Sacraments, which He has appointed in *Remembrance* of Him,
under the *Goſpel*.

And as thoſe who *neglected* or *deſpis'd* the *Sacrifices*, when
they might be had, from the *Legal Prieſts*, according to *God's*
Inſtitution, were made liable to *Death*, and did forfeit their *Ti-*
tle to the Participation of *Chriſt* the *Archi-Type:* So thoſe who
neglect or *deſpiſe* the *Sacraments* which He has commanded as
the *Means* of *Grace*, and of our *Inward* Participation of Him,
under the *Goſpel*, do thereby juſtly forfeit their *Title* to ſuch
Participation.

For, if we will not take *God's* Way, we have no *Promiſe*
nor *Reaſon* to ſecure us in the following of our own Inven-
tions.

SECT. XI.

The Quaker-Objection, *That there are no* Signs *under the* Gospel.

I. THE *Quakers* throw off all *Outward* Institutions, as not only *Useless,* but *Hurtful* to the *Christian* Religion; which, they pretend, consists not only *chiefly* (which is granted to them) but *solely* in the *Inward* and *Spiritual* Part. They say, That all *Figures* and *Signs* are *Shadows;* and that when *Christ,* who is the *Substance,* is come, the others cease of course. That they have attain'd to *Christ* the *Substance;* and therefore these *Shadows* are of no use to them. That *Baptism* and the *Lord's Supper* are some of these *Shadows;* and these were Indulged to the *Early* and *Weak* Christians, but that the *Quakers,* who have stronger Participations of the *Spirit,* are got beyond these *Beggarly Elements,* &c.

II. This is settl'd as a Foundation-Principle, That *no* Figures, *or* Signs, *are perpetual; or of Institution, under the Gospel-Administration, when Christ, who is the Substance, is come; though their Use might have been Indulged to young Converts in Primitive Times.*

A Key, &c. by *W. P.* Printed, 1694. C. 10. of Water-Baptism, and the Supper, P. 24.

Ans. 1. To say they were not *Perpetual,* is one thing; but to say, That they were not so much as *of Institution* under the Gospel, seems a strange Assertion, when *Christ* gave the *Institution* out of his own Mouth, *Matt.* xxviii. 19. *Go Baptize.* And of his *Supper,* said, *This do,* Luk. xxii. 19.

2. The Reason why this shou'd not be *Perpetual,* is very *Precarious,* to suppose that the *Holiness* of any Person shou'd exempt him from observing the *Institutions* of *God;* whereas *Christ* himself submitted to them, and said, That it *became him to fulfil all Righteousness,* i. e. all the Righteous *Institutions* of *God.* This is the Reason which *Christ*   *Mat.* iii. 15.

gave

gave for his *Baptifm*; yet the *Quakers* think that their *Holineß*
will excufe *them* from *Baptifm*. *Chriſt* fubmitted to *John's*
Baptifm, faying, That we ought to fulfil all God's Inftitutions:
Yet the *Quakers* will not fubmit to *Chriſt's Baptifm*, faying, That
they are got beyond it. All were required to fubmit to *John's*
Baptifm, during his *Miniſtry*, becaufe he was fent from God to
Baptize; therefore *Chriſt* alfo fubmitted unto it ; and did receive his own Commiffion to *Baptize*, by the vifible Defcent of
the *Holy Ghoſt*, upon his receiving the *Baptifm* of *John*. All
are yet more exprefly commanded to receive the
Mat.xxviii.19. *Baptifm* of *Chriſt*. Go, *Baptize* ALL NATIONS.
Mar.xvi.15. Go ye into ALL THE WORLD, *and Preach the Go-*
ſpel to EVERY CREATURE : *He that Believeth, and is*
BAPTIZED, ſhall be faved. But the *Quakers* and *Muggletonians*
excufe themfelves, as being too *Good* for it, *They truly feeling in*
themſelves (as it is expreffed in the *Key* before quoted, *p. 26.*)
the very Thing, which outward Water, Bread and Wine do ſignifie,
they leave them off. But were they as *Holy* as they pretend; yet
wou'd not this excufe them from obferving the *Inſtitutions* of
Chriſt; nay, the greateft Sign of *Holineß*, and true *Humility*,
is, not to think our felves above his *Inſtitutions*, but *obediently*
to obferve them, after the Bleffed Example of *Chriſt* our *Lord*.
And it is the greateft Inftance of *Spiritual Pride*, and the moft
Fatal Deception in the World, thus to *over-value* our felves ; it
betrays the groffeft *Ignorance* of *Spiritual* things : For the more
a Man knows of *himſelf*, and of *God*, the more he difcovers of
his own *Weakneß* and *Unworthineß*; he appears *leß* in his own
fight, and frames himfelf the more *Obſequiouſly*, with the moft
profound *Humility* and *Refignation, Dutifully* and *Zealouſly* to obferve every the *leaſt* Command of *God*. They are *Novices* in
the Knowledge of *God*, who are *lifted up with Pride* ; and thefe
fall into the Condemnation of the Devil, 1 Tim. iii. 6.

And what can be greater *Pride*, than to think our felves in
an higher Condition of *Perfection*, than the *Holy Apoſtles*, and
all thofe Glorious *Saints* and *Martyrs*, who were the *Firſt-fruits*
of the *Goſpel*, called (in the *Key* above quoted) by the *Leſſening*
Stile of Young Converts, in Primitive Times?

St. *Paul*, though IMMEDIATELY *Converted*, and *Enlightned*
MIRACULOUSLY from HEAVEN, was commanded to go to *Ana-*
nias

nias to be *Baptized.* But our *Quakers* pafs him off as a *Young Convert,* they have got *beyond him,* and think themfelves' more HIGHLY *Enlightned* than he was : And, for that Reafon only, not to need that *Baptifm,* which was thought neceffary for him.

And all the other *Chriftians,* from *Chrift* to *George Fox,* were *Young Converts !* Then it was that a greater *Light* was given than ever was known in the *Church* of *Chrift* before, to make the *Outward Baptifm* ceafe, as of no longer ufe to thofe who had attain'd the *Subftance !* Or otherwife none of the *Primitive Chriftians* knew their own *Holinefs ;* or were fo *Humble* as not to own it, to that Degree as to place themfelves above all *outward Ordinances !*

Thefe are the Grounds and Reafons of the *Quakers,* why *Baptifm,* and the *Lord's Supper* were not *Perpetual !*

Which, in the mildeft word that I cou'd frame, I have call'd *Precarious.* And they muft appear to be fuch, till the *Quakers* can give fome other Proof befides their own faying fo, either that the *Holinefs* of any Perfon can excufe him from the Obfervance of *Chrift's Inftitution :* Or, that they have a greater *Degree of Holinefs* than all others fince *Chrift,* who have been *Baptized.*

3. But the *Perpetuity* of *Baptifm,* and *the Lord's Supper,* are fully expreffed in the Words of the *Scripture.* When *Chrift* gave Commiffion to his *Difciples* to *Baptize,* he promifed to be with them, in the Execution of that Commiffion, *even unto the End of the World,* Matt. xxviii. 20. which fhews, that the Commiffion was to defcend after the Death of the *Apoftles* to whom it was given. And it tells how long ; *Alway, even unto the End of the World.* The like *Perpetuity* is annexed to the *Inftitution* of *the Lord's Supper,* 1 Cor. xi. 26. Till *Chrift* come again. It was Inftituted in *Remembrance* of him ; and therefore to be continu'd till his *Coming again.*

III. I know the *Quakers* do Interpret this, not of *Chrift's Outward* and *Perfonal* coming at the *Refurrection,* which (after *Hymeneus* and *Philetus,* 2 Tim. ii. 18.) they fay is *paft already,* that is, *Inwardly perform'd,* by the Spiritual Refurrection of *Chrift,* or the *Light* in their *Hearts.* And they fay, That the

Inftitution

Inftitution of the *Lord's Supper* was only to continue till that *Inward Coming*, or forming of *Christ* in our *Hearts*; which they having obtain'd, (as they prefume) therefore they *throw off the Outward Supper*.

But was not *Christ* formed in the Hearts of the *Apoftles*, to whom *Christ* gave his *Holy Supper*; as much as in the Hearts of the *Quakers* now ? Was he not *Come*. SPIRITUALLY to *Paul*, after his Converfion? And before his Command, above quoted, of continuing the Practice of *the Lord's Supper*, till his *Coming*?

If they fay, That this was only to have it continu'd to thofe *weaker* Chriftians, who had not Chrift *thoroughly* formed in their Hearts.

Firft, Who can fay, That Chrift is *thoroughly* formed in his Heart? May there not be greater and greater *Degrees* of the *Infpiration* of Chrift in our Hearts? And can we ever come to the End of it, fo as to need no *further* Infpiration, or *Coming* of Chrift *within us*? Therefore Chrift's *Inward* Coming is *always* to be expected. His *further* and *further Coming* and *Infpiration*.

But if that *Coming*, which the *Quakers* wou'd make to be the Determination of the *Outward Inftitution* of the *Lord's Supper*, be the *Leaft Degree* of his Coming, then every *Chriftian*, nay, according to the *Quakers*, every *Man* in the World, not only is, but always was exempted from the Obfervation of that *Inftitution*; becaufe the *Quakers* do own, That every Man in the World has, and ever had *the Light within*, which they make to be *Chrift*, at leaft, an *Influence* and *Infpiration* from *Chrift*; and fo to be a *Coming*, or *Prefence* of his in the *Heart*: And therefore, by this Rule, Chrift is *Come* to every Man, in fome *Degree* or other : And, if there be not fome *ftinting*, or *afcertaining* of this *Degree*, then *Chrift* was *always* fo *Come* to *All*, as to make the *Inftitution* of the *Lord's Supper* ufelefs, at *all Times*, to *All*. Nay, it was *ended*, before it *began*. For, if his *Inward Coming* does *end* it, it cou'd never *begin*, becaufe he was *always* fo *Inwardly Come*.

But if there are fome *Degrees* of his *Coming* fo *weak* as to need the Help of the *Outward Inftitution*, to which God has annexed the Promife of his *Grace*, when duly *Adminiftred*, and *Receiv'd*, then thefe *Degrees* muft be known, elfe thofe may be depriv'd

of

of the Benefit of it, who have moſt need of it: And thoſe are they who think that they need it leaſt.

Secondly, The *Quakers* do not always pretend, all of them, to the ſame *Degrees* of *Perfection* (if there be *Degrees* in *Perfecti-on*) they muſt be ſenſible ſometimes (at leaſt others are) of the many Weakneſſes of ſome of their Number: Why then do they not allow the *Lord's Supper* to thoſe *Weaker* ones? Elſe they muſt ſay, That it was not intended for the *Weak* more than for the *Strong*. And ſo, that the *Inſtitution* and *Practiſe* of it, by *Chriſt* and his *Apoſtles*, was wholly uſeleſſ, and to *no purpoſe*. And that all thoſe high Things ſaid of it, That it is the *Communion* of the *Body* and *Blood* of *Chriſt*, 1 Cor. x. 16. And *Chriſt's* own Words, *This is my Body*: And therefore, that the receiving it unworthily, is being *Guilty of the Body and Blood of the Lord*: That therefore we ſhou'd approach to it, with the greateſt *Reverence* and *Preparation*, to *Examine our ſelves* ſeriouſly and diligently, that we may receive it with pure Hearts and Minds: And the Dreadful Judgments which do attend the *Neglect*, or *Abuſe* of it, not only *ſundry Diſeaſes*, and divers kinds of *Deaths*, but *Damnation*, 1 Cor. xi. from Ver. 27. I ſay all theſe were Words thrown into the Air, of no Meaning, nor Import at all, if the *Quaker* Interpretation be true, which makes nothing at all of *the Lord's Supper*, but renders it wholly *Precarious* and *Inſignificant*, even at the time of its *Inſtitution*; and now to be *hurtful* and *pernicious*, as drawing Men from the *Subſtance*, to meer *Shadows*; for they make of it *no more!*

IV. But I wou'd beſeech them to conſider how much more highly God does value it; and how Material a part of his Religion he does make it: For when St. *Paul* was taught the Faith immediately from Heaven, and not from thoſe who were *Apoſtles* before him (as he tells us, *Gal.* i. 16, 17.) *Chriſt* took care to inſtruct him as to this of *the Lord's Supper* particularly. And he preſſes it upon the *Corinthians*, as having received it from God. *For I have received of the Lord* (ſays he, 1 Cor. xi. 23.) *that which alſo I delivered unto you, that the Lord Jeſus, the ſame Night in which he was Betrayed, took Bread*, &c. and ſo goes on to relate the whole *Inſtitution* of the *Lord's Supper*, and the mighty Conſequences, the Benefits and Advantages of it; the *Exa-*

mination

mination preparatory to it ; and the *Vengeance* both *Temporal* and *Eternal*, which was due to the *Contempt* of it.

This shews, that *Christ* did not Institute this *Holy Sacrament* by Chance. It was the last Act of his Life ; and his *Dying Bequest* to his *Church* ; fill'd with all his *Blessings*, and carrying with it, to the *Worthy Receivers*, the whole *Merits*, and *Purchase* of his *Death* and *Passion*, the *Remission* of our *Sins*, and full Title to *Heaven* ! *Brethren, I speak after the Manner of Men* ; Gal. iii. 15. *tho' it be but a Man's Testament, yet, if it be confirmed, no Man disannulleth, or addeth thereto.* How much less then can any Man take upon him to *disannul* this *last Will* and *Testament* of *Christ's*, which he has left to his *Church* ; and *Bequeathed* it to her with His *Dying* Breath !

This was the Reason that it was not only so particularly Recorded by the several *Evangelists* in the *Gospels* ; but when St. *Paul* was taught Immediately from *Heaven*, this most Material *Institution* was not forgot, but *Christ* Himself instructed him in it ; to shew the great Stress and Value which He laid upon it.

And let this suffice, to have said in this place, concerning this other Sacrament of *the Lord's Supper*. Its *Institution* is as Plain and Express as that of *Baptism*. And the *Practise* of it, in the Days of the *Apostles*, and all Ages since has been as *Universal*. And what has been said of *Baptism*, is of Equal Force as to this : And the *Quaker* Arguments against this, are upon the same Foundation as those against *Baptism* ; only they have not so many Objections against this : Therefore I have made *Baptism* the chief Subject of this Discourse ; yet so, as likewise to Include the *Sacrament* of *the Lord's Supper*. Therefore we will go on to consider what remains of the present Objection (which Militates equally against both) that there are no *Signs* under the *Gospel.*

V. And here let me observe,

First; That these *Signs* and *Figures* which the *Quakers* make Incompatible to the *Gospel* State, ought only to be understood of the *Signs* and *Figures* in the *Law*, which were ordain'd as *Types* of *Christ*. And of these it is truly argu'd, That when *Christ*, who is the *Substance*, is come, they must cease of course ; which Argument the *Quakers* bring against the *Signs* and *Figures* which

which *Christ* did Institute under the *Gospel*. But how foreign this is from their purpose, let any one judge. For those *Signs* and *Figures* which were appointed by *Christ*, cou'd not be *Types* of *Christ*; because a *Type* is what goes *before* a Thing, and shews it *to come*. And therefore, when that which it *foreshews* is come, it ceases. But, as there were *Types* under the *Law* to *foreshew* Christ's coming in the *Flesh*, and his *Sacrifice* upon the *Cross*, which therefore are ceased; so *Christ* has appointed other *Types* to foreshew his *second coming* to Judge the World; and which therefore must last till he shall so come, as the *Types* of his *first coming* did last, till he did so come. The *Sacrifices* under the *Law*, did *præfigure* the *Death of Christ*; but the *Sacraments* under the *Gospel*, were Instituted in *Remembrance* of it; as well as for *Types* of our future *Union* with *him* in *Heaven*. Therefore the same Reason which makes the *Legal Types* to *cease*, does infer, That the *Evangelical Types* must *not cease*, till they likewise shall be *fulfilled*; which will not be till we arrive at *Heaven*. Thus, as they are *Types*. And then,

Secondly, As they are *Remembrances* of what is past, they are to last as long as the *Remembrance* of that which they *Represent* ought to last with us. *Christ* did not Institute *his Supper*, that we shou'd thereby *Remember* his *Death*, a *Day*, or a *Year*, but till his *Coming again*. His *Death* took his *Personal* Presence from us; and therefore till that Return, we must continue the *Remembrance*, that is, of his *Absence*, till the Glorious Return of his *Visible Body*, which was separated from us by his *Death*.

Thus no advantage can be brought to the *Quaker* Pretences against the *Christian Sacraments*, from the *Sacrifices* and other *Signs* or *Figures* under the *Law*.

VI. We come now to Examine, what they set up against any *Signs* or *Figures* under the *Gospel*, from another Topick; and that is, That the *Gospel* is all *Substance*, and therefore that there must be no *Sign* or *Figure* at all in it.

Answ. By *Substance* here they mean that which is *Inward*, or *Spiritual*, that every thing in the *Gospel* is *Spiritual*.

But this will overthrow all *outward*, or *Bodily* Worship. For that is distinguished from *Spiritual*, or *Inward* Worship.

And, in one sense, all *Bodily* Worship is a *Sign* or *Figure* of the *Inward*, or *Spiritual*; which is the *Principal* and *Substantial* Worship. Thus *Bowing* the *Knee*, or *Uncovering* the *Head* at *Prayer*, are *Signs* or *Figures* of the *Inward Reverence* and *Devotion* of the *Heart*.

And this the *Quakers* practise; therefore, by their own Argument, they have *Signs* and *Figures* as well as others; only they throw off those of *Christ*'s Inftitution, and make new ones of their own.

It is impossible to be without *Signs* and *Figures*. For this whole World is a *Figure* of that which is to come. We our selves are *Figures* of *God*, being *Images* of him: And what is an *Image* but the *Figure* or *Sign* of a Thing? *Christ* is a *Figure* of *God*, being *the Express Image of his Person*, Heb. i. 3. And we now have the Knowledge of God *in the Face of Jesus Christ*. God is a *Light* Inaccessible to *Angels*, as well as unto *Men*, without some *Medium*: His *Essence* cannot be seen or known *Immediately*, by any but *Himself*. All *Creatures* partake of him in *Signs* and *Figures* of him; each in their several Degrees; there are *Higher* and more *Noble Figures*; but all are *Figures*. And God has, in all Ages, through the World, Difpenfed himfelf to Mankind in *Signs* and *Figures*; we cou'd not otherwife apprehend Him. *Christ* is the moft *Noble* and *Lively Figure* of *God*: Therefore his Difpenfation is far beyond all others that went before him. Yet even now, *We fee through a Glass darkly*, 1 Cor. xiii. 12. or, *in a Riddle*; as our *Margent* reads it, ἐν αἰνίγματι, in a *Figure*.

What is *the Bible* that we read, what are *Words* but the *Signatures*, the *Signs* or *Figures* of *Things*? We can fee the *Effence* of no one thing in the World, more than of *God*. And what are all thofe *Accidents* of *Colour*, *Quantity* and *Quality*, by which we diftinguifh Things, but fo many *Figures*, or *Signs* of them?

So very wild is that Notion, that there muft be no *Signs* or *Figures* under the *Gofpel*!

It would be much *Truer*, if they had faid, That there are nothing elfe but *Signs* and *Figures*: There is nothing elfe without a *Figure* but *God*! For all *Creatures* are *Figures of Him*, *Christ*, the *Higheft*.

But

But have the *Quakers* no *Figures*? *G. Fox* in his *Saul's Errand*, p. 14. fays, That *Christ's Flesh* is a *Figure*. They call the *Body* of *Christ* generally, a *Figure*, a *Vail*, a *Garment*. Then either they have none of it, or they have *Figures*.

Richard Hubberthorn wrote, That *Christ's coming in the Flesh was but a Figure :* He meant of the *Inward* coming of *Christ*, or the *Light* in the Heart, which they call the *Substance* and the *Mystery* ; of which *Christ's Outward coming* in the *Flesh*, they fay, was but a *Shadow*, or the *History* (to use their own words.) *G. Fox* made a great *Mystery*, or *Figure* of his *Marriage*, which, he faid, *Was above the State of the first* Adam, *in his Innocency* ; *in the State of the second* Adam *that never fell.* He wrote, in one of his General *Epistles* to the *Churches*, (which were read, and valu'd by the *Quakers*, more than St. *Paul's*,) That his Marriage was a *Figure* of the *Church coming out of the Wilderness.* This, if deny'd, I can Vouch undeniably, but it will not be deny'd, tho' it be not Printed with the reft of his Epiftles, but I have it from fome that read it often. But why was it not Printed ? That was a fad Story. But take it thus. He Marry'd one *Margaret Fell*, a Widdow, of about *Threescore* Years of Age; and this *Figure* of the *Church* muft not be *Barren* ; therefore, tho' fhe was paft Child-bearing, it was expected, that, as *Sarah*, fhe fhou'd miraculoufly Conceive, and bring forth an *Ifaac*; which *G. Fox* promis'd and boafted of; and fome that I know have heard him do it, more than once. She was call'd, *The Lamb's Wife.* And it was faid amongft the *Quakers*, That the *Lamb* had now taken his *Wife*, and fhe wou'd bring forth an *Holy Seed.* And Big fhe grew, and all things were provided for the *Lying in* ; and, he, being perfwaded of it, gave notice to the Churches, as above obferv'd. But, after long waiting, all prov'd *Abortive*, and the *Figure* was fpoil'd. And now you may guefs the Reafon, why that *Epiftle* which mention'd this *Figure*, was not *Printed.*

I wou'd have brought nothing into this Difcourfe that looks like a *Jeft* ; but they have compelled me. And it may be of ufe to them, to fhew them, that while they throw off the *Sacraments* of *Christ's* Inftitution, upon the Pretence that there muft be no *Signs* or *Figures* under the *Gofpel*, they, at the fame time

Snake in the Grafs, 1st Part, pag. 208.

2d Part, p. 43.

time, make Ridiculous *Signs* and *Figures* of *G. Fox*, and his Fantaftical *Marriage* ; and of feveral other things ; every thing almoft among them, is a *Sign* or *Figure* of fomething to come upon the World. How many of their *Lying Prophets* have call'd themfelves *Signs* to the Men of their Generation, as the *Holy Prophets* were in their Day ?

VII. There have been *Outward Signs*, in all the Inftitutions of Religion, fince the beginning of the World ; as well *before*, as *under* the *Law*, and now under the *Gofpel*. Only they have been *vary'd*, or *Ended* according to what they præfigur'd. Thus thofe *Signs* which had no further Tendency, than to point out what *Chrift* did or fuffer'd upon *Earth*, are *fulfill'd* and there-fore *Ended*.

But there were fome *Signs*, which, though they pointed to *Chrift* upon *Earth*, had yet a further Tendency : For *Signs* may be appointed to more Ends than one. Thus the Inftitution of the *Sabbath* was appointed for the Commemoration of God's *Reft* from the Works of the *Creation*, *Gen*.ii.3. and *Exod*.xx.11. and likewife the reft of the Children of *Ifrael* (who were the *Type* of the *Church*) from their *Captivity* and *Slavery* in *Egypt*, *Deut*. v. 15. (which expreffes the Servitude of *Sin* and *Hell*) and their final *Reft* in *Canaan* (the Type of *Heaven*) after their for-ty Years wandering in the *Wildernefs*, (which reprefent the La-bours of this Life.) But this was not the Ultimate *Reft*, or *Sab-bath*, Heb. iv. 18. *For if* Jofhua *had given them Reft, then wou'd he not afterward have fpoken of another Day ; there remain-eth therefore* σαββατισμὸς, *the keeping of a Sabbath* (which fignifies *Reft*) *to the People of God.* *For he that is entred into his Reft, he alfo hath ceafed from his own Works, as* God *did from his.* Thus *Chrift*, as he fuffered the 6th Day of the Week, the fame Day that *Man* was *created*, and *fell*; fo, on the fame Day on which God Refted from his Work of *Creation*, *viz*. the 7th Day, did *Chrift* Reft in his Grave, from his Work of *Redemption*. And there is yet a farther *Reft* or *Sabbath* beyond this ; and that is, the Eternal *Reft* in *Heaven*, Heb. iv. 11. *Let us labour therefore to enter into that Reft*.

Now, though feveral Significations of the *Sabbath* are alrea-dy paft, as the Deliverance out of *Egypt* ; the Entrance into
Canaan ;

Canaan ; and the *Reſt* of *Chriſt,* in his *Grave :* Yet there being one behind, that is the *Sabbath* of *Heaven,* therefore do we ſtill keep the *Sabbath* as à *Type* of it.

But there is another Reaſon for the Continuance of the *Sabbath* ; and that is, That it was not only ordained as a *Type* of Things to come ; but as a Commemoration of what was paſt, *viz.* Of *God's Reſt* from his Works of *Creation.* And, by the Alteration of the *Day* of the *Sabbath,* it ſerves likewiſe to us *Chriſtians,* as a Commemoration of the *Reſurrection* of *Chriſt,* and his Conqueſt over the Powers of *Death* and *Hell.* It was the *firſt Day* in which *Light* was created; and *Chriſt* (who is our *True Light,* of which the *Viſible Light* is but a *Shadow,* and was ordain'd as a *Type) Aroſe* from the *Dead,* the *ſame Day* ; and gave *Light* to thoſe who ſat in *Darkneſſ,* and the *Shadow* of *Death,* by the Joyful Tidings of our *Redemption* from *Hell,* and *Eternal Bliſſ* in *Heaven !*

Now ſo long as the Works of our *Creation* and *Redemption* are to be kept in Memory, ſo long is the *Sabbath* to continue, as à Commemoration of theſe Ineſtimable Benefits.

And, by the ſame Reaſon, ſo long as we ought to commemorate the *Death* and *Paſſion* of our *Lord* ; ſo long ought the *Sacrament* of it to continue ; which he Inſtituted in Remembrance of it ; and commanded it to be continu'd till his *Coming again.*

Thus you ſee that there are *Signs* under the *Goſpel* ; not only the two *Sacraments* of the *Church* (which flowed diſtinctly out of *Chriſt's* Side, after his *Death,* upon the *Croſs)* but that the *Goſpel* does ſtill retain the *Signs* of *Commemoration,* which have deſcended down to us all the way from the *Creation :* And likewiſe ſuch *Signs* or *Types* as have yet a Proſpect forward, and are not wholly fulfill'd.

And 3*dly,* The *Signs* of *Preſent Signification,* as the *outward* Acts of *Worſhip:* To which we are as much, nay more ſtrictly obliged under the *Goſpel,* than they were under the *Law.* As St. *Irenæus* argues, *(adverſ. Hæreſ.* l. 4. c. 34.) That the manner of *Worſhip,* as of *Sacrifices,* is chang'd : but not the *Worſhip* aboliſhed. *Non Genus oblationis Reprobatum eſt, oblationes enim & illic, oblationes autem & hic : Sacrificia in Populo, Sacrificia & in Eccleſia ; ſed Species-Immutata eſt tantum.* i. e. The
Kind

Kind or *Nature* of the *Offering* is not *Abolished*; for there were *Offerings* under the *Law*, and there are *Offerings* also under the *Gospel*: there were *Sacrifices* among the People of the *Jews*. There are *Sacrifices* likewise in the *Church*: but the *Species* or *Manner* of them only is changed, *viz*. That some *Sacrifices* under the *Law* were *Bloody*, as Præfiguring the *Death* of *Christ*: and therefore that *Sort* or *Manner* of *Sacrificing* is ceased, because *Fulfill'd* in the *Death* of *Christ*: But their *Un-bloody Sacrifices*, and *Oblations*, as of *Tythes*, and other *Offerings* Remain still among *Christians*: and are *Signs*, as much as they were under the *Law*. The *outward Worship* of God must be by Actions proper and significant. *Nihil enim Otiosum, nec sine Signo, nec sine Argumento apud eum.* i. e. *For there is nothing Empty, nor without a Sign, nor without Signification in the Worship of God.* And, in the very next words, he applies this to *Tythes*. *Et propter hoc illi quidem Decimas —— And for this reason the Jews paid Tythes, viz.* as a *Sign* of their *Dependence* upon *God*, and having Receiv'd All from Him: And in Hopes of their Receiving More from Him. *Sed nos omnia——* But the *Christians*, instead of a *Tenth* Part, which the *Jews* gave, Give *All* that they have, because (says he) they have a *Better Hope*. And, *ch. 27.* shewing how *Christ* did *Heighten* the *Law*, as, instead of *Adultery*, to forbid *Lust*; instead of *Murder*, to forbid *Anger*; and, instead of giving the *Tythe*, commanding to sell *All*: And this, says he, *is not a Dissolving of the Law, but Enlarging it.* So that no Part of the *Law* is *Destroy'd*; and *All* is not *Fulfill'd*; and since *All* must be *Fulfill'd*, it follows, that what is not yet *Fulfill'd*, must yet *Remain*: And Many of the *Signs* in the *Law* not being *Fulfill'd* in *Christ's Death*, nor ever to be *Fulfill'd* while we Live upon this Earth, consequently do *Remain*, and must so Remain to the End of the World. So that the *Gospel* has *Signs* as well as the *Law*; and, in Great Part, the same *Signs*; with other *Sacramental Signs* added by *Christ*, which are those of which we now Treat, *Baptism*, and *The Supper* of *The Lord*.

Iren. ibid.

Matth. v. 17, 18.

VIII. And let us Reflect, that ever since God made *outward* Things, and gave us this *Body*, as the *Soul* does act by the Mediation of the *Body*; so has God ordain'd, that his *Gifts* and

Graces

Graces fhall be convey'd to us by *Outward Signs* and *Means*.

Chrift us'd *outward Signs* and *Means* for his *Miraculous Cures*; to fhew, that tho' the *Vertue* did not come from the *Means*, yet that they were of Ufe, and not to be Defpifed.

But why do we fay, that the *Vertue* does not come from the *Means*? We fay fo, when we cannot tell the *Reafon* and *Manner* how the *Means* work their *Effect*, and can we tell it, in thofe which we call *Natural* Means? No furely, we know only by *Obfervation*, and *Experience*; and what often comes to pafs, we call it *Natural*, as being the common Courfe of Things; not that we know the Reafon of it, more than of thofe Occurrences which we call *Miraculous* and *Extraordinary*.

Man doth not live by Bread alone, but by every Word that proceedeth out of the Mouth of God.

Bread has no Vertue of its own to *nourifh*; but only what it receives from *God*: And if he give his *Vertue* (for it is *His only*) to a *Stone*; or any thing elfe, it will *nourifh*: And *Bread* will, and does ceafe to *nourifh*, when he withdraws his *Bleffing* from it.

Therefore the *Spittle* of *Chrift* and the *Clay*, the *Waters* of *Siloam* and *Bethefda*, and the *Brazen-Serpent* had as great Vertue to Cure, when they were Appointed by *God*, as *Bread* has to *nourifh*; and the Vertue came as much from *Them*, as it does from the *Bread*, in our Daily Food.

Now, if the *Brazen-Serpent*, which was but a *Type* of *Chrift*, had Vertue to Cure the *Body*; fhall we deny that the *Bread*, which *Chrift* bleffed, for the *Remiffion* of *Sin*, has Vertue to work that Effect?

He whofe fingle *Fiat* made the Worlds, and whofe Influence gives Power to all Things, and makes them what they are; he faid of that *Bleffed Bread*, THIS IS MY BODY. And his Holy Apoftle faid of it, *The Bread which we break, is it not the Communion of the Body of Chrift?* And do we doubt, how it works this Effect? Dare we Reject it, becaufe it feems ftrange to us, how it fhou'd work this Effect, who know as little how our *Daily Bread* does nourifh our *Bodies*? Do we object our Ignorance how a Man can be *Born* of *Water* and the *Spirit*, who can give as fhort an Account how we are formed, of a drop of *Water*, in the Womb; and by what Ligaments fuch different *Natures*

I *tures*

tures as *Soul* and *Body*, are compacted and linked together? How can we pretend to have *Faith* in *Chrift*, and yet not believe his *Words*, because of the seeming difficulty to our Underftandings (who know nothing) of the *Method* and *Manner*, how He can bring them to pafs?

According to our *Faith* it will be unto us. Therefore let us *Humble* our *Souls* greatly, and imitate the *Holy Angels* (far more *Enlight'ned* than we are) who *vail* their *Faces* before *God*; and prefume not to difpute his Commands; or pretend to underftand all the *Methods* of his *Power* and *Wifdom* unfearchable! but *defire to look into thofe Things*, 1 Pet. i. 12. thofe Glorious *Myfteries* of the *Gofpel*, which the *Quakers* defpife, as below the *Meafure* to which they have attain'd! And the *Principalities and Powers in Heavenly places*, do fubmit to *learn* the *Manifold Wifdom of God*, Ephef. iii. 10. from that *Church*, which the *Quakers* do *vilifie* and *trample under their feet*; as thinking it uncapable to teach them any thing, or to adminifter to them the *Sacraments* which *Chrift* has commanded.

But becaufe the Difpute will arife which that *Church* is, in the miferable Divifions of *Chriftendom*, and amongft the various forts of the Pretenders to it, I have in the Difcourfe mention'd in the *Advertifement*, I hope, given a plain and 'fure Rule to guide all *Honeft* and *Difinterefted* Enquirers, in that moft *neceffary* and *fundamental* Point.

The

The Conclusion.

Shewing the Neceffity *of* Water-Baptifm.

THE Sum of what has been faid, concludes in the great Neceffity there is of *Water-Baptifm.*

But before I fay more of it, I will obviate an Objection, which may arife from the word *Neceffary.*

If it be *Abfolutely* Neceffary, then none can be *faved* without it: Which fort of *Neceffity* I do not plead for. This is plainly diftinguifhed in the *Catechifm* of *our Church,* where *this,* and the *other Sacrament* (of the *Lord's Supper).* are faid to be *Generally* neceffary to *Salvation. Generally,* that is, in the *General* and *Common* Methods which are prefcribed in the *Gofpel.* For no Body will pretend to *Limit* GOD; as if HE cou'd not *fave* by what *Means* and *Methods* HE pleafes. But we are ty'd up to thofe *Rules* which HE has Prefcribed to *Us* : Yet *We* muft not Tie HIM up to thofe *Rules,* to which HE has Ty'd *Us.*

But who are they who have Reafon to expect God's *Extraordinary* Mercies, out of the *Common* Methods of Salvation; and to be made Partakers of the *Inward,* without the *Outward* Baptifm?

I. Thofe who being confcientioufly concern'd for the *Outward,* yet cannot obtain it, through the Want of a *Minifter* of *Chrift,* Lawfully *Ordain'd* to Adminifter it; as in *Turkey, Africa,* &c.

Thefe are under an *Invincible Neceffity :* And their *Earneft Defires* (I doubt not) will be accepted by *God*; and the *Spiritual* Baptifm be confer'd upon them, without the *Outward.*

II. Thofe who have been *Baptifed* by Perfons, not lawfully *Ordain'd,* and confequently they have receiv'd *no Baptifm,* having receiv'd it from thofe who had no Commiffion to *Admini-*

fter

fter it ; but who were Guilty of the Higheſt *Sacrilege*, in Uſurp-ing ſuch a Sacred Commiſſion, not Lawfully Deriv'd to them by a *Succeſſive Ordination* from the *Apoſtles :* But yet, through a General Corruption of the Times, ſuch *Baptiſms* are ſuffer'd to paſs, whereby the Perſons ſo *Baptized*, ſwiming down the Stream, do think their *Baptiſm* to be valid, and therefore ſeek not for a *Re-Baptization* from thoſe who are truly Empowred to Adminiſter it! I ſay, Where no ſuch *Re-Baptization* is taught, and thereby the People know nothing of it ; in ſuch Caſe, their *Ignorance* is, in a Manner, *Invincible* ; and their *Sincerity* and *Devotion* in Receiving *No Sacraments*, yet thinking them *True Sacraments*, may be Accepted by *God*, and the *Inward Grace* confer'd, and the *Defects* in the *Outward* and *Viſible Signs* may be *Pardon'd*.

But neither of theſe Caſes does reach thoſe, who *neglect* the *Outward Means*, upon Pretence of *Inward Perfection* without them. Theſe *Deſpiſe* the *Ordinance* of *Chriſt*, and make them-ſelves *Wiſer* than *He* ; as if *He* had appointed *Means* either *Un-neceſſary*, or *Ineffectual* to the *Ends* for which they were in-tended !

And I deſire theſe to conſider the *Great Neceſſity* there is for *Water-Baptiſm*, as before Explain'd.

1. Becauſe it is ordain'd as the *Means* whereby the *Inward Baptiſm* of the *Holy-Ghoſt* is given , as I before quoted , *Acts* ii. 38. Be *BAPTIZED, and ye ſhall Receive the Gift of the HOLY GHOST*. By *This Baptiſm*, cou'd not be meant the *Baptiſm* with the *Holy Ghoſt*, becauſe *This Baptiſm* is Here propoſed as the *Means* whereby to Receive the *Inward Baptiſm* of the *Holy Ghoſt*.

Again, *Epheſ.* v. 26. *That He* (Chriſt) *might Sanctifie and Cleanſe it* (the Church) *with the Waſhing of Water, by the Word.* Here the *Waſhing* of *Water* is the *Means*, tho' the *Operation* and *Vertue* is from the *Word :* And therefore the *Outward Waſhing* or *Baptizing* (which means the ſame, as before told, *Sect.* 1.) cannot be the ſame with the *Word* in this *Text*.

2. *Chriſt* having appointed this as the *Means*, you ſee what *Streſs* He lays upon it, and how *Neceſſary* He makes it.

John iii. 5. *Except a Man be Born of Water and the Spirit, he cannot Enter into the Kingdom of God.* Here the *Water* and
the

the *Spirit* are plainly Diſtinguiſhed, and *Both* made *Neceſſary* to *Salvation*, the *Outward* as well as the *Inward*: As it is written, *Rom.* x. 10. *For with the Heart Man Believeth, unto Righteouſneſs; And with the Mouth Confeſſion is made unto Salvation.* The Belief of the Heart is *Neceſſary* unto *Righteouſneſs, i.e.* to make Us *Righteous* before *God*: But the *Outward Confeſſion* of the *Mouth* is likewiſe as *Neceſſary* to our *Salvation*. As *Chriſt* ſaid, (*Matt.* x. 32.) *Whoſoever ſhall Confeſs me before Men*, &c. We muſt *Outwardly*, and *before Men*, Confeſs to Chriſt, by the Due Performance of His *Outward Ordinances*; without which our *Inward Belief* in Him will not be ſufficient to our *Salvation*. *Baptiſm* is an *Outward Badge* of *Chriſtianity*, by being the *Outward Form*, appointed to admit Men as *Members* of the *Church of Chriſt*; and whereby they own themſelves to be ſuch, *before Men*: But thoſe who will not wear this *BADGE*, as a *Confeſſion* to Chriſt, before *Men*; Chriſt will not Confeſs them, before His *Father*, in *Heaven*.

Mark xvi. 16. *He that Believeth and is Baptized, ſhall be ſaved.* Here both the *Outward* and the *Inward* are join'd together, and both made *Neceſſary*; For, by *Baptiſm*, Here, cannot be meant the *Inward Belief*, that wou'd make a Tautology of the *Text*, and mean thus, *He that Believeth and Believeth* —— Thus it muſt be, if by *Baptiſm*, in this Text, the *Inward Baptiſm*, or *Belief* of the *Heart* be meant. But this being plainly meant of the *Outward Baptiſm*, the Conſequeuce from this Text is plainly this, That *he who doth not Believe, and is not* Baptized, *ſhall not be Saved.* Of which I adjure the *Quakers* to Conſider moſt ſeriouſly: For tho' they had the *Inward Baptiſm* as much as they Pretend to it, yet were the *Outward* neceſſary. *Peter* thought *Water* neceſſary to give *Outward Baptiſm* to thoſe who had already Received the *Inward Baptiſm* of the *Holy Ghoſt*, Acts x. 47.

And the *Doctrine of Baptiſm* is reckon'd among the *Principles* and *Foundations* of *Chriſtianity*, together with *Faith* and *Repentance*, &c. *Heb.* VI. 1, 2.

But the *Quakers*, like *Naaman*, flout at the *Means*, as too *eaſie* to be *effectual*; and call *Baptiſm*, in contempt, *Water-Sprinkling*, And I will anſwer them with *Naaman*'s Servants, (2 *Kings* V. 13.) *If Chriſt had bid thee do ſome great thing, wouldſt*

wouldſt thou not have done it? How much rather then when *He faith to thee, Waſh and be Clean?* And as *neceſſary* as the *Waters* of *Jordan* were to the *Cleanſing* of *Naaman*, ſo *neceſſary* are the *Waters* of *Baptiſm* to the *Cleanſing* of our *Souls*. None dare ſay, that G O D cou'd not have Cleanſed *Naaman* otherwiſe: But G O D having, by his *Prophet*, appointed that Means, if *Naaman* had neglected it, he had not otherwiſe been Cured. How much more, when G O D has appointed the Means of *Baptiſm*, by his *Son*, if we *Neglect* it, ſhall we be Sav'd without it? *He that Deſpis'd* Moſes's *Law, dyed without Mercy: Of how much ſorer Puniſhment, ſuppoſe ye, ſhall he be thought worthy, who hath trodden under foot the* Inſtitution *of the* Son *of* G O D, *and counted it an unholy thing, doing Deſpight to it,* Inventing *Contemptible Names* for it, and *Ridiculing* the *Adminiſtration* of it? But as the S*pirit* of *God moved,*at firſt, *upon the Face of the Waters* (Gen. 1. 2.) to *Impregnate* them, and make them *Fructiſie*; and gave a *Miraculous* Vertue to the *Waters* of *Jordan*, of *Siloam*, and *Betheſda*, for Healing of the *Fleſh*; Why ſhou'd we Doubt that the ſame S*pirit* can and will S*anctiſie* the *Waters* of *Baptiſm* to the *Myſtical Waſhing away of Sin*, having the Poſitive *Inſtitution* and *Promiſe* of *Chriſt* for it? *Acts* II. 38. *Repent and be Baptized, every one of you, in the Name of Jeſus Chriſt, for the Remiſſion of Sins, and ye ſhall Receive the Gift of the Holy Ghoſt.*

This was not the *Extraordinary Gift* of *Miracles*, which is here Promiſed,(and which all *Baptized* Perſons did not *Receive* or *Expect*) but the *Remiſſion of Sins*. And let me add, That the *Ordinary Saving Graces* of the *Spirit*, which work *ſilently*, without *Obſervation* or *Show*, are much Preferable, and more Deſirable, than the *Extraordinary Gift* of *Miracles*, which, for a time, were Neceſſary, at the firſt Propagation of the *Goſpel*; and held Men's Eyes in Great Admiration: But were of Dangerous Conſequence to the Poſſeſſors, and a *Temptation* often to *Vanity*; which had almoſt over-ſet the Great *Apoſtle*, 2 Cor. xii. 7, 8, 9. and threw others into the Pit of Deſtruction, *Matth.* vii. 22, 23. 1 *Cor.* xiii. 2. and therefore were not to be *Pray'd* for, or *Deſir'd*: We muſt be totally *Paſſive* in this Caſe; and when ſent, being for the Conviction of others, to Receive ſuch an *Extraordinary Gift*, with *Fear* and *Trembling*, leſt it Hurt

our

our *weak Minds*, not capable, but by as *Extraordinary* an Affi-
ftance of *Divine Grace*, to Bear fuch mighty *Revelations*, and
not to let in with it a fecret *Pride* in our felves; which fpreads
our *Sails* fo wide, that without a Proportionable *Ballaft* of deep
Humility, we fhall be driven from our *Compaß*.   The Enemy
throws in this ftrong *Temptation*, with thofe *Miraculous Gifts*;
which *vain* Men do *Ignorantly* Covet, and fome falfly *Pretend*
to, to their own *Deftruction*.   But much more *Valuable* are
thofe Saving *Graces*, which we are commanded Daily to *Pray*
for, and Daily to *Endeavour:* Much more *Available* to us, and
Precious in the fight of God, than all *Miraculous Gifts*, is that
Gift of *The Holy Ghoft*, the *Remiffion of Sins*, which is Promis'd to the Due Reception of *Baptifm*, and enrolls our *Names*
in Heaven.   *Behold* (faid *Chrift* to his *Difciples*,
who *Boafted*, that *even the Devils were fubject to*   Luk. x. 17, 18,
them, through His Name) *I give unto you Power*   19, 20.
to tread on Serpents and Scorpions, and over all the Power of the
Enemy; and nothing fhall, by any means, hurt you; notwithftand-
ing in this Rejoice not, that the Spirits are fubject unto you; But
rather Rejoice, becaufe your Names are written in Heaven.

To be added to the End of Sect. VIII. p. 34.

But *R. Barclay* argues in his *Apology*, That the *Baptifm*, of
which the *Ark* was a *Type*, cou'd not be the *Outward*, or *Water-*
Baptifm, becaufe that it felf is a *Type*, *viz.* Of the *Inward* or
Spiritual Baptifm.   And he fupports this Notion by a *Criticifm*
upon the Word 'Ἀντίτυπον in this Text, which he fays is not
rightly Tranflated in our *Englifh* by *The like Figure*.   Becaufe,
he fays, the Word 'Ἀντίτυπۃ fignifies the thing *Typify'd*, and
not the *Type*.

But, by his leave, it fignifies the quite contrary. *Heb.*ix. 24.
not the thing *Typify'd*, but only the *Type*: For there the *Holy*
Places made with Hands are call'd the 'Ἀντίτυπα, the *Figures* or
Types of the *True*.   And that Word is not to be found, except
in thefe two Texts, in the whole New Teftament.   And therefore

fore if one of these Texts must explain the other, the Word Ἀντίτυπος, or *Anti-Type*, 1 *Pet*. iii. 21. must be taken in the same Sense, in which it is used, *Heb*. ix. 24. because there it cannot possibly be taken to mean the thing *Typify'd*, or the *Archi-Type*; therefore neither ought it to be so strain'd, as *Barclay* does, to mean the quite contrary, in the present Text. And our Translation is Justify'd, which renders Ἀντίτυπος *the like Figure*, as does the *Vulgar*, *Similis formæ*. For both the *Waters* of the *Ark*, and of *Baptism*, are the *outward* and *visible Signs*, but not the thing *signify'd*, which is the *Salvation* of the *Soul*, by the *Re-generation* and *Washing* of the *Spirit*. And they are like *Figures*, both signifying the same thing, in a manner very *like* to one another. That as *Noah*, &c. were sav'd in the *Ark* by *Water* from *Corporal Death*, so are the True Believers sav'd by the *Water* of *Baptism*, from the *Death* of *Sin* and *Hell*. In which Sense the *Ark* was a *Type* of the *outward* or *Water-Baptism*, tho' both were *Types*, but one nearer than the other. And because the *Baptism* mentioned in this Text, 1 *Pet*. iii. 21. is an Ἀντίτυπος, a *Type* or *Figure*; therefore it must be the *Outward* and *Water-Baptism*, which is here meant. For the *Inward* and *Spiritual Baptism* is not the *Type* or *Figure*, but the thing *signify'd*. And thus *Rob. Barclay*'s Argument and *Criticism* has turn'd into a full Demonstration of the direct contrary of that for which he brought it: And has thoroughly Established the *Divine Institution* of the *Outward* or *Water-Baptism*.

July 17.
1696.

FINIS.

A
DISCOURSE;

SHEWING,

Who they are that are now Qualify'd to
Administer *Baptism* and the *Lord's-Supper*.

Wherein the Cause of

EPISCOPACY

Is briefly Treated.

By the Author

O F

A DISCOURSE

Proving the Divine Institution of *Water-Baptism*.

No Man taketh this Honour unto himself, but he that is called of God, as was Aaron, Heb. 5. 4.

LONDON,

Printed for *C. Brome* at the *Gun*, at West-end of St. *Paul's*; *W. Keble-white* at the *Swan* in St. *Paul's* Church-Yard; and *H. Hindmarsh* at the *Golden-Ball* over-against the Royal Exchange, *Cornhill,* 1698.

THE
PREFACE.

THIS *Difcourfe* was Promis'd in that which I formerly Publifh'd, proviug the *Divine Inftitution* of *Water-Baptifm*; And was intended to have been Annex'd to that, but fome Delays prevented it.

I can give no good Reafon why it has ftay'd thus long, having made but little Addition to what was then done: But other things Interven'd, and, as it is ufual in Delays. the firft in Defign proves the laft in Fact.

The Subject of this has led me directly upon the larger Theme of *Epifcopacy*; which having been fo *Elaboratly* and fo *Often* treated of, I intend not in this to Branch out into fo wide a Field; but in a fhort compendious Method, to lay before the *Quakers*, and others of our *Diffen-*
ters,

ters from *Epifcopacy*, the Heart of the Caufe, fo far particularly as it concerns our prefent Subject, the *Right* of *Admimiftring* the Sacraments of *Chrift*.

And to avoid the length of Quotations, when brought into the Difcourfe, and Dilated upon, I have, at the end, Annex'd a fmall *Index* of Quotations out of the Primitive *Fathers* and *Councils* of the firft 450 Years after *Chrift*, to which the Reader may Recur, as ther is occafion. And having them all in one view, may confider them more Intirely, and Remember them the better.

I have Tranflated them for the fake of the *Englifh* Reader, but have put the *Originals* in another *Column*, to juftifie the Tranflation; and for their fakes who may not have the Books at hand.

The CONTENTS.

The Contents.

IV. If

The Contents.

The Contents.

A

A DISCOURSE

Shewing, who they are that are now qualify'd to Administer BAPTISM, and the LORD's SUPPER.

SECT. I.

The Necessity of an Outward Commission to the Ministers of the Gospel.

Some *Quakers* having perus'd my *Discourse* of *Baptism*, think the *Quaker* Arguments against it sufficiently Answered: And they have but one Difficulty remaining, that is, who they are (among the various Pretenders) that are duly Qualify'd to *Administer* it.

And if satisfaction can be given to them herein, they promise a perfect Compliance to that *Holy Institution*.

The Chief thing they seem to stand upon is the *Personal Holyness* of the *Administrator*; thinking that the *spiritual* Effects of *Baptism* cannot be convey'd by the means of an *Unsanctify'd Instrument*.

But yet they Confess, that there is something else Necessary, besides the *Personal Holiness* of the *Administrator*: Otherwise, they wou'd think themselves as much *Qualify'd* to *Administer* it as any others; because, I presume, they suppose themselves to have as great a Measure of the *Spirit* as other Men.

This *Requisit* which they want, is that of *Lawful Ordination*.

But the *Presbyterians*, *Independents*, and *Baptists* do pretend to this. Therefore their *Title* to it is to be Examin'd.

B   And,

And, that we may proceed the more clearly in this Matter, with Respect still to that Difficulty upon which the *Quakers* lay the stress; we will Inquire concerning those *Qualifications* which are Requisit in any Person that shall take upon him to *Administer* the *Sacraments* of *Christ*'s Institution. And,

These Qualifications are of two sorts, *Personal* or *Sacerdotal*.

I. *Personal.* The *Holiness* of the *Administrator.* And, though this is a great Qualification to *Fit* and *Prepare* a Man for such an Holy Administration, yet this *Alone* does not sufficiently Qualifie any Man to take upon him such an Administration.

II. But there is moreover requir'd, 2ly. A *Sacerdotal* Qualification, that is, an *Outward Commission*, to Authorize a Man to execute any *Sacerdotal* or *Ministerial* Act of Religion. For, *This Honour no Man taketh unto himself, but he that is called of God, as was* Aaron; *so also Christ glorify'd not himself to be made an High-Priest; But he that said unto him, thou art my Son*——*Thou art a Priest,* &c.

_{Heb. v. 4.}

Accordingly we find that *Christ* did not take upon Him the Office of a *Preacher*, till after that *Outward Commission* given to Him by a *Voice* from *Heaven*, at His *Baptism*; for it is written, *Matth.* iv. 17. *From that time* Jesus *began to Preach*: Then He *Began*; and He was then *about Thirty Years of Age*, Luke iii. 23. Now no Man can doubt of *Christ*'s Qualifications, before *that time*, as to *Holiness*, *Sufficiency*, and all *Personal* Endowments. And if all these were not sufficient to *Christ* Himself, without an *Outward Commission*, what other Man can pretend to it upon the Account of any *Personal* Excellencies in Himself, without an *outward Commission* ?

III. And as *Christ* was outwardly Commissioned by His *Father*, so did not He leave it to His Disciples, every ones Opinion of his own sufficiency, to thrust himself into the *Vineyard*, but Chose Twelve *Apostles* by Name; and after them, Seventy others of an Inferior Order, whom He sent to *Preach*.

IV. And as *Christ* gave *outward Commissions*, while He was upon the Earth, so we find that His *Apostles* did Proceed in the same Method, after His Ascension. *They ordained them Elders in every Church.*

_{Act. xiv. 23.}

V. But had they, who were thus Ordained by the *Apostles*, Power

Power to Ordain others? Yes, *For this cause left I thee in Crete, that thou shouldest —— Ordain Elders in every City. Lay hands suddenly on no Man,* &c. St. *Clemens,* in his first *Epistle* to the *Corinthians,* writing concerning the *Schism* which was then risen up amongst them, says, Parag. 44. *That the Apostles fore-knowing there wou'd be Contests concerning the Episcopal Name (or Office) did themselves appoint the Persons.* And not only so, lest that might be said to be of force, only during their time. But that they *afterwards established an Order how, when those whom they had Ordained shou'd Die, others, fit and approved Men, shou'd succeed them in their Ministry.* Par. 43. *that they who were intrusted with this Work, by God, in Christ, did Constitute these Officers.*

Tit. 1. 5
1 Tim. v. 22.

Καὶ οἱ Ἀπόσολοι ἡμῶν ἔγνωϛ διὰ τ̃ Κυείε Ἰησᾶ Χεɩσᾶ, ὅτι ἔεɩς ἔϛαι ἐπὶ τ̃ ὀνόματ⊙ τῆς Ἐπισκοπῆς. διὰ ταύτἳ ἐν τῇ αὐτἳ πρόγνωσιν εἰληϕότες τελείαν, κατέϛησ τὰς πϱοειϱημϑύ ς, & μεταξύ, ἐπινομὴν δεδώκασιν, ὅπως ἐὰν κοιμαϑῶσιν, διαδέξων〕 ἕτεϱοι δεδοκιμασμϑ́νοι ἄνδϱες, τὴν λειτεϱγίαν αὐτῶν. — οἱ ἐν Χεɩϛῷ πιϛεύϑντες πρὸς Θεᾶ ἔϱγον τᾶτο, κατέσι τὰς πϱοειϱημϑ́νας.

But this Matter depends not upon the Testimony of him, or many more that might be produced. It is such a Publick Matter of Fact; That I might as well go about to quote particular Authors, to prove that there were *Emperors* in *Rome,* as that the *Ministers* of the *Church* of *Christ* were *Ordained* to succeed one another; and that they did so succeed.

SECT. II.

The Deduction of this Commission is continu'd in the Succession of Bishops and not of Presbyters.

BUT there is a Dispute, whether this *Succession* was preserv'd in the Order of *Bishops* or *Presbyters?* or whether both are not the same.

I. *Answ.* 1. This is the Contest betwixt the *Presbyterians* and us: But either way it operates against the *Quakers,* who allow of no *Succession* deriv'd by *outward Ordination.*

I. *Answ.*

II. *Anfw.* 2. But becaufe the *Defign* of this *Difcourfe* is to fhew the *Succeffion* from the *Apoftles*, I anfwer that this *Succeffion* is preferv'd and deriv'd only in the *Bifhops*: As the continuance of any *Society*, is deduc'd in the *Succeffion* of the *Chief Governors* of the *Society*, not of the *Inferior Officers*. Thus in *Kingdoms*, we reckon by the *Succeffion* of the *Kings*, not of *Sheriffs* or *Conftables*; and in *Corporations* by the *Succeffion* of the *Mayors* or other *Chief Officers*; not of the Inferiour *Bailiffs* or *Serjeants*: So the *Succeffion* of the *Churches* is Computed in the *Succeffion* of the *Bifhops*; who are the *Chief Governours* of the *Churches*; and not of *Presbyters*, who are but *Inferiour Officers* under the *Bifhops*.

III. And, in this, the Matter of Fact is as Clear and Evident as the Succeffion of any *Kings* or *Corporations* in the World.

To begin with the *Apoftles*, we find not only that they Conftituted *Timothy* Bifhop of *Ephefus*, and *Titus* of *Crete*, as in the Subfcriptions of St. *Paul's* Epiftles to them: But, in *Eufebius* and other *Ecclefiaftical Hiftorians*, you have the *Bifhops* Nam'd who were Conftituted by the Apoftles themfelves, over the then famous Churches of *Jerufalem, Antioch, Rome*, and *Alexandria*, and many other Churches; and the *Succeffion* of them down all along.

St. *Polycarp*, Bifhop of *Smyrna*, was Difciple to St. *John* the *Apoftle*; and St. *Irenæus*, who was Difciple to St. *Polycarp*, was Conftituted *Bifhop* of *Lyons* in *France*.

I mention this, becaufe it is fo near us; for, in all other *Churches*, throughout the whole World, where-ever *Chriftianity* was Planted, *Epifcopacy* was every where Eftablifh'd, without one Exception, as is Evident from all their Records.

And fo it was with us in *England*, whither it is generally fuppos'd, and with very good Grounds, that St. *Paul* firft brought the Chriftian Faith. *Clemens Rominus*, in his *Firft Epift.* to the *Corinthians*, Paragr. 5. Says, that St. *Paul* went Preaching the Gofpel to the fartheft bounds of the *Weft*; ἐπὶ τὸ τέρμα τῆ Δύσεως. by which Term *Britain* was then Underftood. And *Theodoret* exprefly Names the *Britains* among the Nations Converted by the *Apoftles*. (To. 4. ferm. 9. p. 610.) And *Eufebius* in his *Evangelical Demonftration*, (l. 3. c. 7. p. 113.) Names likewife the *Britains*, as then Converted.

But

But whether St. *Paul*, or, as some Conjecture, *Joseph* of *Ari-mathea*, or any other *Apostolical* Person was the first who Preach-ed *Christ* in *England*, it matters not, as to our Present Pur-pose; who Enquire only concerning *Episcopacy*; And it is Cer-tain by all our Histories, that as far up as they give us any Account of *Christianity* in this *Island*, they tell us likewise of *Bishops*; and the Succession of this *Church* of *England* has been Deduc'd in the Succession of *Bishops*, and not of *Presbyters*. And particularly in the *Diocess* of *London*, which was the first *Archi-Episcopal See*, before *Augustin* the *Monk* came hither, af-ter which it was Establish'd in *Canterbury*. And the *Saxon* Writers have Transmitted the Succession of their *Bishops* in *Can-terbury*, *Rochester*, *London*, &c.

And in Countries so Remote and Barbarous as *Island* it self we find the same care taken; *Ara* or *Aras* an *Islandish* Priest Surnam'd *Hinfrode* the *Learned*, who flourish'd in the *Eleventh Century*, and was 25 Years Old when *Christianity* was brought thither, in his Book of that Country written in *Islandish*, has Transmitted to Posterity, not only the *Succession* but the *Genea-logies* of the *Bishops* of *Skalholt* and *Hola* (the two Episcopal Sees of *Island*) as they Succeeded one another in his Time. I mention this of *Island*, to shew that *Episcopacy* has Extended it self Equally with *Christianity*, which was carry'd by it, into the Remotest Corners of the Earth; upon which account the *Bishops* of *Skalholt* and *Hola*, and their *Succession*, are as Remark-able Proofs of *Episcopacy*, tho' not so Famous as the *Bishops* of *Canterbury* and *London*.

IV. If the *Presbyterians* will say (because they have nothing left to say) that all *London* (for Example) was but one *Parish*; and that the *Presbyter* of every other *Parish* was as much a *Bishop* as the *Bishop* of *London*; because the words Ἐπίσκοπος and Πρεσβύτερος *Bishop* and *Presbyter* are sometimes us'd in the same sense; They may as well prove that *Christ* was but a *Deacon*, because He is so call'd, *Rom.* xv. 8. Διάκονος, which we rightly Translate a *Minister*: And *Bishop* signifies an *Overseer*, and *Presbyter* an *Ancient Man*, or *Elder Man*; whence our Term of *Alderman*. And this is as good a Foundation to Prove that the *Apostles* were *Aldermen*, in the *City* acceptation of the Word; or that our *Aldermen* are all *Bishops* and *Apostles*; as to Prove that *Pres-*

byters

byters and *Bishops* are all one, from the Childish *Gingle* of the Words.

It wou'd be the same thing, if one shou'd undertake to Confront all Antiquity, and Prove against all the Histories, that the *Emperors* of *Rome* were no more than *Generals* of *Armies*, and that every Roman *General* was *Emperor* of *Rome*, because he cou'd find the word *Imperator* sometimes apply'd to the *General* of an *Army*.

Or as if a *Common-wealth-man* shou'd get up, and say, that our former *Kings* were no more than our *Dukes* are now; because the Stile of *Grace*, which is now given to *Dukes*, was then given to *Kings*.

And suppose that any one were put under the Pennance of Answering to such Ridiculous Arguments; what Method wou'd he take, but to shew that the *Emperors* of *Rome*, and former *Kings* of *England*, had *Generals* of *Armies* and *Dukes* under them, and Exercis'd Authority over them?

Therefore when we find it given in Charge to *Timothy*, the first *Bishop* of *Ephesus*, how he was to Proceed against his *Presbyters*, when they Transgressed; to Sit in *Judgment* upon them, Examine *witnesses* against them, and pass *Censures* upon them, it is a most Impertinent *Logomachy* to argue from the *Etymology* of the Words, that notwithstanding of all this, a *Bishop* and a *Presbyter* are the same thing. Therefore that one Text, 1 *Tim.* v. 19. is sufficient to silence this Pitiful Clamour of the *Presbyterians*; our *English* reads it, *against an Elder*, which is the *Literal* Translation of the word Πρεσβύτερ, κατὰ πρεσβυτέρου, *against a Presbyter receive not an Accusation, but before two or three witnesses, and, them that sin Rebuke before all, that other's also may fear.* Now, upon the *Presbyterian* Hypothesis, we must say that *Timothy* had no *Authority* or *Jurisdiction* over that *Presbyter*, against whom he had Power to Receive *Accusations*, Examine *witnesses*, and pass *Censures* upon him: And that such a *Presbyter* had the same *Authority* over *Timothy*—which is so Extravagant and against Common Sense, that I will not stay longer to Confute it; and think this enough to have said concerning the *Presbyterian* Argument from the *Etymology* of the words *Bishop* and *Presbyter*.

And

And this likewise Confutes their other *Pretence*, which I have mention'd, that the Ancient *Bish pricks* were only *Single* and *Independent Congregations*, or *Parishes*. This is a *Topick* they have taken up but of late (being Beaten from all their other Holds) and Launched by Mr. *David Clarkson*, in a Book which he Entitules *Primitive Episcopacy*; which has given occasion to an Excellent Answer, by Dr. *Hen. Maurice*, call'd *A Defence of Diocesan Episcopacy*, Printed 1691. which, I suppose, has ended that Controversie, and hindred the World from being more troubl'd upon that Head. And their other little Shift, and as Groundless, that the Primitive *Bishops* were no other than their *Moderators*, advanced more lately by *Gilb. Rule* late *Moderator* of the *General Assembly* in *Scotland*, has been as *Learnedly*, and with great Clearness of *Reason*, Confuted by the Worthy *J. S.* in his *Principles of the Cyprianick Age*, Printed 1695.

But, as I said, that Text, 1 *Tim.* v. 19. has made all these *Pretences* wholly useless to the *Presbyterians*: For supposing their most Notorious false supposition, as if the *Bishopricks* of *Jerusalem*, *Rome*, *Alexandria*, or *London*, consisted but of one single Congregation, and that such *Bishops* had no *Presbyters* under them; but that all *Presbyters* were Equally *Bishops*; I say, supposing this, then it must follow from what we Read of *Timothy*, that one *Bishop* or *Presbyter* had *Jurisdiction* over other *Bishops* or *Presbyters*, which will Destroy the *Presbyterian* Claim of Parity, as much as their Confession to the *Truth*, and plain *Matter of Fact*, that *Bishops* had *Presbyters* under their *Jurisdiction*; and that they were Distinct *Orders*: Notwithstanding that a *Bishop* may be call'd Διάκονος a *Deacon*, or *Minister* of *Christ*; and likewise πρεσβύτερος, an *Elder* or *Grave* Man, which is a Term of *Magistracy* and *Dignity*, and not ty'd to *Age*. And a *Presbyter* may likewise, in a found Sense, be call'd a *Bishop*, that is, an *Overseer* or *shepherd*, which he truly is over his Particular Flock; without denying at all his Dependance upon his *Bishop* and *Overseer*:

V. As under the Term of *Priest*, the *High-Priest* was Included, without Destroying his *Supremacy*, over the other *Priests*. Against which *Korah* and his *Presbyters*, or Inferiour *Priests* arose. And if the *Presbyterians* will take his word, whom, of all the Fathers, they most Admire, and Quote often on their side, that is, St. *Jerom*, he will tell them, in that very E-

piſtle (ad *Evagr.*) which they Boaſt favours them ſo much, That what *Aaron*, and his *Sons*, and the *Levites* were in the *Temple*, that ſame are *Biſhop*, *Presbyter*, and *Deacon* in the *Church*.

And long before him, *Clemens Romanus* in his 1 *Epiſt.* to the *Corinthians*, makes frequent Alluſion to the *Epiſcopacy* of the *Levitical Prieſthood*, and argues from thence to that of the *Chriſtian* Church. Thus Paragraph 40. Τῷ ϑ᾽ Ἀρχιερεῖ ἰδίαι λειτȣργίαι δέ-
To the High-Prieſt (ſays he) *were* δομέναι εἰσὶ· ἡ τοῖς Ἱεροῖσιν ἴδι@ ὁ
allotted his proper Offices; to the τόπ@ πρȣστακ᾽), ἡ Λαΐταις ἰδίαι
Prieſts, their proper place was aſ- διακονίαι ᾔκειν᾽· λαϊκὸς ἄνθρωπος
ſigned; and to the Levites their τοῖς λαϊκοῖς πρȣτάγμασιν δέδε᾽·
ſervices were appointed; and the Lay-men were Reſtrain'd within the precepts to Lay-men. And Paragraph 42, he applies that Scripture, *iſa. LX. 17.* to the Officers of the *Chriſtian* Church, and renders it thus; *I will Conſtitute their Biſhops in Righteouſneſs, and their Deacons in Faith.* The *Greek* Tranſlation of the LXX has it thus. *I will give thee Rulers* (or Princes) δώσω τὰς ἄρχοντάς σȣ ἐν εἰρήνῃ, ἡ *in Peace; and thy Biſhops in Righteouſneſs.* τὰς Ἐπισκόπȣς σȣ ἐν δικαιοσύνῃ.

It was the frequent Method of theſe Primitive Fathers to Reaſon thus from the Parallel 'twixt the *Law* and the *Goſpel*, the one being an Exact *Type* of the other, and therefore being fulfill'd in the other. And in this they follow'd the Example of *Christ*, and the *Apoſtles*; who argu'd in the ſame manner, as you may ſee *Matth.* v. *1 Cor.* x. the whole *Epiſtle* to the *Hebrews*, and many other Places of the *New Teſtament.*

VI. Now the *Presbyterians* are deſir'd to ſhew any one Diſparity betwixt their Caſe and that of *Korah*; who was a Prieſt of the *ſecond* Order, that is, a *Presbyter*; and withdrew his Obedience from the *High-Prieſt* with other Mutinous *Levites*: For, ther was no matter of *Doctrine* or *Worſhip* betwixt them and *Aaron*, nor any other Diſpute but that of *Church-Government*. And, by the Parallel betwixt the *Old Teſtament* and the *New*, *Korah* was a *Presbyterian*, who Roſe up againſt the *Epiſcopacy* of *Aaron*. But this Caſe is brought yet nearer home; for, we are told (*Jude* xi.) of thoſe under the *Goſpel*, who periſh in the gain-ſaying of *Korah*: And in the *Epiſt.* of *Clem. Rom.* to the *Corinthians*, before Quoted, Paragraph 43. He plainly applys this Caſe of *Korah*, to the ſtate of the *Chriſtian Church*; ſhewing at large, that as *Moſes*, by the

Com-

Command of God, Determin'd the Pretenfions of the Twelve *Tribes* to the *Glory* of the *Prieſthood*, by the Miraculous Budding of *Aaron's* Rod, which was after the *Schiſm* and *Puniſhment* of *Korah* and his Company. So *likewiſe*, he ſays, the *Apoſtles* fore-knowing, by *Chriſt*, that Diſſentions wou'd ariſe alſo in the *Chriſtian Church*, by various Pretenders to the *Evangelical Prieſt-hood*, did Settle and Eſtabliſh, not only the Perſons themſelves; But gave *Rules* and *Orders* for continuing the *Succeſſion* after their Deaths, as I have before Quoted his Words. So that it is plain from hence, That the *Evangelical Prieſthood*, is as *Poſitively*, and *Certainly* Eſtabliſh'd, and Determin'd, in the *Succeſſion* of *Eccleſi-aſtical Ordination*, as the *Levitical* was, in the *Succeſſion* of *Aaron*. And conſequently, that the *Rebellion* of *Presbyters* from under the Government of their *Biſhops*, is the ſame Caſe as the *Rebellion* (for ſo it is call'd, *Numb.* xvii. 10.) of *Korah* and his *Levites*, a-gainſt *Aaron*; who had as good a Pretence againſt him from the word *Levite*, which was Common to the whole *Tribe*; as the *Presbyterians* have againſt *Biſhops*, from the Name *Biſhop* and *Presbyter*, being us'd ſometimes promiſcuouſly, and apply'd to the *Clergy* in General; which is a Term that Includes all the *Or-ders* of the *Church*, as *Levite* did among the *Jews*.

VII. But, to leave the fruitleſs Conteſt about *words*, let this Matter be Determin'd, as other Matters of Fact are.

If I pretend to ſucceed any Man in an *Honour* or *Eſtate*, I muſt name him who had ſuch an *Eſtate* or *Honour* before me; and the Man who had it before him; and who had it before him; and ſo up all the way to him who firſt had it; and from whom all the reſt do derive; and how it was lawfully deduc'd from one to another.

This the *Biſhops* have done, as I have ſhewn; and can name all the way backward, as far as Hiſtory goes, from the Preſent *Biſhop* of *London*, (for example) to the firſt Plantation of *Chriſtianity* in this Kingdom: So, from the preſent *Biſhop* of *Lyons* up to *Irenæus* the Diſciple of St. *Polycarp*, as before is told. The Records are yet more certain in the Great *Biſhopricks* of *Rome*, *Antioch*, *Alexandria*, and others, while they laſted in the World: And tho' the Records may not be Extant of every ſmall *Biſhoprick*, which was leſs taken notice of; as the Names of many *Kings* are loſt, in obſcure Nations; of many *Mayors* or *Sheriffs*, who, notwithſtanding have as cer-

tainly

tainly Succeeded one another, as where the Records are Preferv'd. I fay, tho' every *Bifhop* in the World cannot tell the Names of all his *Predeceffors* up to the *Apoftles*, yet their *Succeffion* is certain : And in moft Chriftian Nations there are *Bifhops* who can do it; which is a fufficient Proof for the reft, all ftanding upon the fame Bottom, and being Deriv'd in the fame Manner.

Now, to Ballance this, it is Defir'd, that the *Presbyterians* wou'd fhew the Succeffion of any one *Presbyter* in the World; who was not likewife a *Bifhop*, in our acceptation of the Word, in the like manner, from the *Apoftles*.

Till when, their fmall *Criticifms* upon the *Etymology* of the Words, *Bifhop* or *Presbyter*, is as poor a Plea, as if I fhou'd pretend to be Heir to an Eftate, from the likenefs of my Name to fomebody who once had it.

And here I cannot choofe but apply the Complaint of our *Saviour*, *John* v. 43. If any come, in the Name of *Chrift*, that is, by a Commiffion from Him, deriv'd down all the way, by Regular *Ordination*, him ye will not Receive : Nay, tho' he be otherwife a Man without Exception, either as to his *Life* and *Converfation*, or as to his *Gifts* and *Sufficiency* for the *Miniftry*; you make this his *Commiffion* an *Objection* againft him: For that *Reafon alone*, you will not accept him. But, if another come in *his own Name*, that is, with no *Commiffion*, but what he has from himfelf; his *own Opinion* of his *own Worthinefs*; *giving out that himfelf is fome Great One*, (Act. viii. 9.) him ye will Receive, and Follow and Admire him; *Heaping to your felves Teachers, having Itching Ears*, as it was Prophefy'd of thefe moft degenerate Times, *2 Tim.* iv. 3.

But as to thofe well-difpos'd *Quakers*, for whofe Information Chiefly I have wrote this *Difcourfe*, I muft fuppofe that their Inquiry is wholly concerning the feveral *Titles* of *Bifhops*, *Presbyterians*, *Independents*, &c. to the true *Succeffion* from the *Apoftles*: That it may *thereby* be known, to which of all thefe they ought to go for *Baptifm*.

This I have fhewn, in behalf of *Epifcopacy*; and put the *Presbyterians* to prove their *Succeffion*, in the Form of *Presbytery*, which they can never do: Becaufe, as I have faid before, the *Chronology* of the *Church* does not Compute from the *Succeffion* of the

Presbyters,

Presbyters, but only of the *Bishops*, as being the *Chief Governors* of the *Church*. And therefore, tho' in many *Bishopricks*, the *Roll* of their *Bishops* is preserv'd from the *Apostles* to this Day; yet there is not one bare *Presbyter*, that is, the *Minister* of a *Parish*, and no more, no not in all the World, who can give a *Roll* of his *Predecessors*, in that *Parish*, half way to the *Apostles*, or near it: For, from the first Plantation of *Christianity*, the *Church* was Divided into *Bishopricks*; this was necessary for the *Government* of the *Church*: But it was not so early Sub-divided into *Parishes*. The *Presbyters*, at first, attending upon the *Bishop*, were sent out by him, to such *Places*, and for such *Time* as he thought fit; and Returning, gave Account of their *stewardships*, or were *Visited*, and *Changed* by him, as he saw Cause: And therefore, tho' one might come after another, in the Place where he had *Ministred* before; yet they cou'd not *Properly* be said to *Succeed* one another; as (to speak Intelligibly to the *Quakers*) many of them do Preach after *G. Fox*, yet none of them are said to *Succeed* him.

I have been thus long upon the *Presbyterians*, because they only, of all our *Dissenters*, have any *Pretence* to *Succession*. And what I have said, as to them, must Operate more strongly against the later *Independent*, *Baptist*, &c. who have not the Face to Pretend to *Succession*, but set up merely upon their own pretended *Gifts*.

VIII. But what are these *Gifts*, which they so Highly *Boast*?

1. An *Inward*, and more than *Ordinary* Participation of the *Graces* of the Holy *Spirit*.

2. A *Fluency* and *Powerfulness* in *Preaching* and *Praying*.

I know of no other *Gifts* that any of our *Dissenters* pretend to; unless they will set up for *Miracles*, as *G. Fox*, &c. And other *Dissenters* did likewise pretend to the same, at their first setting out, to amuse the People; but (as the *Quakers*) have let it drop afterwards, to stop any further Examination of it; having already serv'd their Turn by it.

But, as to these pretended *Gifts*, if we may trust to our *Saviour's* Rule, of knowing the *Tree* by its *Fruits*, we cannot think it the *Holy* Spirit of which these Men did partake, who fill'd these *three Nations* with *Blood* and *Slaughter*; and whose *Religion* was never otherwise Introduc'd, than by *Rebellion*, in any Country whither-soever it has yet come.

And

And as to that *Volubility* of *Tongue*, which they Boaft, as the main *Proof* of their *Miffion*, we have found it by Experience, that a little *Confidence* and *Cuftom*, will Improve very flender *Judgments*, to great *Readinefs* in that fort of *Talent*.

And the *Powerfulnefs* which is found in it by fome, who are affected with a Difmal *Tone*, *Wry Faces*, and Antick *Geftures*, is not *more* but *lefs*, if there be either *Method* or *Senfe* in the *Difcourfe*: Which fhews their *Paffion* to proceed not from *Reafon*, but *Imagination*.

The *Scots Presbyterian-Eloquence* affords us *Monftrous* Proofs of this; but not fo many, as you may have from *Eye* and *Ear-Witneffes*.

Such *Courfe*, *Rude*, and *Nafty* Treatment of *God*, as they call *Devotion*; as in it felf, it is the higheft *Affront* to The *Divine Majefty*; fo has it Contributed, in a very great Meafure, to that wild *Atheifm*, which has always attended thefe fort of *Infpirations*: It feeming to many, more Reafonable to Worfhip no *God* at all, than to fet up one, on purpofe to *Ridicule* Him.

But this fort of *Enthufiafm* prefumes upon a *Familiarity* with *God*, which breeds *Contempt*, and Defpifes the *Sobriety of Religion*, as a low Difpenfation. I Recommend to the Reader that Excellent *Sermon*, upon this Subject, of Dr. *Hicks*, call'd *The Spirit of Enthufiafm Exorcis'd*. And I defire thofe to confider, who are moft taken with thefe feeming Extraordinary Gifts of *Volubility* and *Nimblenefs* in *Prayer*, that the moft *wicked* Men are capable of this Perfection; none more than *Oliver Cromwell*, efpecially when he was about fome *Nefarious Wickednefs*: He continu'd moft *Fluently* in this *Exercife*, all the time that his *Cut-throats* were *Murthering* of his *Royal Mafter*. And his *Gift* of *Prayer* was greatly Admir'd. *Major Weir* of *Edinborough*, was another great Inftance, who was ftrangely Ador'd for his *Gifts*, efpecially of *Prayer*, by the *Presbyterians* in *Scotland*; while, at the fame time, he was wallowing in the moft *Unnatural* and *Monftrous* Sins. See his Stupendous Story in *Ravillac Redivivus*.

There are many Examples of this Nature, which fhew that this *Gift* is attainable by *Art*. Dr. *Wilkins* (the Father of the *Latitudinarians*) has given us the *Receipt*, in his *Gift of Prayer*.

Yet none of the Performances of thefe *Gifted-men* are any ways Comparable (as to the wonderful *Readinefs* in which they Boaft) to to the *Extempore Verses* of *Weftminfter School*, which *Ifaac Voffius* cou'd not believe to be *Extempore*, till he gave the *Boys* a *Theme*, which was *fenes bis Pueri*, and he had no fooner fpoke the Words, but he was immediately Pelted with Ingenious *Epigrams* from four or five Boys.

So that this *Volubility* in *Prayer*, which is the *Gift* our *Diffenters* do moft Glory in, may be deduc'd from an *Original* far fhort of *Divine Infpiration*.

But fuppofe that they had really thofe wonderful *Gifts* which they pretend to, yet were this no ground at all to Countenance or Warrant their makeing a *Schifm*, upon that Account.

This Cafe has been Rul'd in a Famous and moft Remarkable Inftance of it, which God was pleas'd to permit, (for the future Inftruction of His Church) at the firft fetting out of the *Gofpel*, in the very Days of the *Apoftles*.

Then it was that *Chrift*, having *Afcended up on High*, gave many and *miraculous Gifts* unto Men; which was neceffary towards the firft Propagation of His *Gofpel*, in Oppofition to all the Eftablifhed *Religions* and *Governments* then in the World, and under their Perfecution.

But thefe *Gifts* of *Miracles* did not always fecure the Poffeffors from *Vanity*, and an high Opinion of themfelves, to the difparagement of others; and even to break the *Order* and *Peace* of the *Church*, by advancing themfelves above their *Superiors*; or thinking none *Superior* to themfelves.

The Great *Apoftle* of the *Gentiles* was not free'd from the *Tentation* of this; whom the *Meffenger of Satan was fent to buffet, leaft he fhou'd be Exalted above meafure, thro' the Abundance of the Revelations which were given to him*, 2 Cor. xii. 7. Nay more, our Bleffed *Saviour* tells of thofe who had *miraculous Gifts* beftow'd upon them, and yet fhou'd be finally *Rejected*, Matth. vii. 22, 23. Therefore He Inftructs His Difciples not to Rejoyce in thofe *Miraculous Gifts* which he beftow'd upon them, but rather *that their Names were written in Heaven*, *Luke* x. 20. which fuppofes, that they might have fuch *Gifts*, and yet their *Names* not be written in *Heaven*.

And when He taught them how to *Pray*, He added no Petition for fuch *Gifts*, but only for the Remiffion of their *Sins*, and the *Sanctifying Graces* of the Holy *Spirit*; which are, as moft *Profitable* to *Us*, fo moft *Precious* in the fight of *God*.

Now

Now some who had thefe *Miraculous Gifts* made ill ufe of them, and occafion'd a great *Schifm* (the firft in the *Chriftian* Church) at *Corinth.* They were *Exalted* above *Meafure,* in their own *Gifts*; and therefore Refus'd to fubmit themfelves to thofe who were their *Superiors* in the *Church* (who, perhaps, had not fuch *Gifts* as they had) but fet up for themfelves, and drew Parties after them, who were Charm'd with their *Extraordinary Gifts*; thinking that the Participation of the *faving Graces* of the Holy Spirit muft there Chiefly be Communicated, where God had beftow'd fuch *wonderful Gifts.* And they laid more ftrefs upon the *Perfonal Qualifications* of thefe *Minifters* of *God,* than upon the obfervance of that *Order* and *Conftitution* which He had Commanded; which was, in Effect, preferring *Men* to *God,* and trufting to the *Inftruments* rather than to the *Author* of their *Religion*; as if thro' the *Power* and *Holinefs* of the *Adminiftrators* of God's *Inftitutions*, and not from *Him* alone, the *Graces* which were Promis'd to the due Obfervance of them, were convey'd. *Act.* iii. 12.

And this, as it turn'd Men from *God,* to Truft in *Man,* fo, as a neceffary Confequence of it, it begot great *Emulations* among the People for one *Teacher* againft another, even (fometimes) when it was not the Fault of the *Teachers.* For People being once let loofe from *Government* and *Order,* to follow the *Imaginations* of their own *Brain,* will run farther than their firft *Seducers* did Intend; and will Carve for themfelves.

Thus, in the *Schifm* of the *Church* at *Corinth,* one was for *Paul,* another for *Apollos,* another for *Cephas,* &c. much againft the Minds of thefe good *Apoftles*; but having been once unfettl'd by the *Pride* and *Ambition* of *Seducers,* they *Heaped to themfelves Teachers, having itching Ears*; and made *Divifions* among themfelves, Pretendingly in behalf of *Chrift* and His *Apoftles,* but in Effect, tending to Divide *Chrift* and His *Apoftles,* as all *Schifms* do.

Againft thefe St. *Paul* Difputes with wonderful force of *Reafon* and *Eloquence*; particularly in the xii *Chap.* of his firft *Epiftle* to thefe fame *Corinthians*; wherein, from the Parallel of the *Unity* of *Members* in the fame *Body,* he admirably Illuftrates, That the many Different and *Miraculous Gifts* which were then Difpenfed all from the fame *Spirit,* cou'd be no more an Argument for any to Advance himfelf beyond his own Station in the *Church,* than for one *Member* of the *Body,* tho' an *Eye* or a *Hand,* the moft *Ufeful* or *Beautiful,*

to

to Glory it felf againft the *inferior Members* (who are all Actuated by the fame *Soul*) or not to be Content with its *Office* and *Station* in the *Body*, and due *Subordination* to the *Head*. Thence the *Apoftle* goes on, and makes the Application in the xiii*th. Chap.* That the moft Exalted *Spiritual* or even *Miraculous Gifts* cou'd not only not Excufe any *Schifm* to be made in the *Body*, that is, the *Church*; But that if any who had fuch *Gifts*, did not employ them for the Prefervation of the *Unity* of the *Church*, which is very properly Exprefs'd by *Charity*, i.e. *Love* for the whole *Body*, fuch *Gifts* wou'd *Profit* him *Nothing*, loofe all their *Vertue* and *Efficacy*, as to the *Poffeffor*, and be rather an *Aggravation* againft him, than any *Excufe* for him, to withdraw his Obedience from his lawful *Superiors*, and Ufurp the Office of the *Head*; and fo make a *Schifm* in the *Body*, upon the account of his *Gifts*; which tho' they were as great as to fpeak with the *Tongues* of *Men* and *Angels*; to underftand all *Myfteries*, and all *Knowledge*; to have all *Faith*, even to Remove *Mountains*; and fuch a *Zeal* as to give all his *Goods* to the *Poor*, and his very *Body* to be *Burned*, yet, if it be done in *Schifm*, out of that *Love* and *Charity* which is due to the *Body*, and to its *Unity*, all is *Nothing*, will profit him nothing at all.

And no wonder, when all that *Heavenly Glory* in which *Lucifer* was Created, cou'd avail him nothing, when he *kept not his firft Principality*, but Afpir'd *Higher*, and made a *Schifm* in the *Hierarchy* of *Heaven*. **Jude 6.**

How then fhall they who have (as St. *Jude* expreffes it) *left their own Habitation*, or *Station* in the *Church*, and advanc'd themfelves above their *Bifhops*, their lawful *Superiors*, the *Heads* and *Principles* of *Unity*, next and immediately under *Chrift*, in their Refpective *Churches*, upon pretence of their own Perfonal *Gifts* and *Qualifications*, and thereby make a *Schifm* in the *Terreftrial Hierarchy* of the *Church*; which is the *Body* of *Chrift*, the *Fulnefs* of him who *Filleth all in all*: How fhall they be Excus'd for **Eph. 1. 23.** this, whofe pretended *Gifts* are in nothing *Extraordinary*, except in a *Furious Zeal* without *Knowledge*, and a *Volubility* of *Tongue*, which proceeds from a Habit of *Speaking* without *Thinking*; and an *Affurance* that is never out of *Countenance* for Ten Thoufand *Blunders*, which wou'd *Dafh* and *Confound* any Man of *Senfe* or *Modefty*, or that confider'd the *Prefence* of *God*, in which he fpoke?

If.

If those truly *Miraculous* Gifts, which were made a Pretence for the *Schifm* at *Corinth*, were not fufficient to juftifie that *Schifm*: How *Ridiculous* and much more *wicked* is the *Pretence* of our Modern *Gifted-men*, who have pleaded their Delicate *Gifts* as a fufficient Ground for all that *Schifm* and *Rebellion* which they have Rais'd up amongft us?

If the real *Gifts* and *Infpirations* of the Holy S*pirit* were *Stinted* and *Limited* by the *Governors* of the *Church*, to avaid *Schifm* and *Confufion* in the *Church*: If the *Prophets* were *Confin'd* as to their Number, to *Two*, or at the moft *Three* at a time; fome ordered to *hold their Peace*, to give place to others; others to *keep filence* for want of an *Interpreter*; and the *women* (tho' *Gifted* or *Infpir'd* as many then were) totally *filenc'd* in the *Church*, or *Publick Affemblies*: What S*pirit* has Poffefs'd our *Modern Pretenders* to *Gifts*, that will not be fubject to the *Prophets*, nor to the*Church*, nor to any *Inftitutions* whether *Divine* or *Humane*! But if their *Superiors* pretend to *Direct* them in any thing, they cry out, what! will you *ftint* the S*pirit*! And think this a fufficient Caufe to break quite loofe from their *Authority*, and fet up an open *Schifm* againft them, upon Pretence of their wonderful *Gifts* forfooth!

I Cor. xiv. from v. 26.

I Tim. II. 12.

That firft *Schifm* in the *Church* of thefe *Corinthians* was vigoroufly oppos'd by the *Apoftles* and *Bifhops* of the *Church*, at that time. They, like good *watch-men*, wou'd not give way to it, knowing the fatal Confequences of it.

This produc'd *Two Epiftles* from St. *Paul* to the *Corinthians*, and *Two* to them from St. *Clement*, then *Bifhop* of *Rome*, which are preferv'd, and handed down to us. It was this fame occafion of *Schifm*, which fo early began to Corrupt the *Church*, that led the Holy *Ignatius* (who flourifh'd in that fame Age) to prefs fo Earneftly in all his *Epiftles* to the feveral *Churches* to whom he wrote, the Indifpenfable obligation of a ftrict *Obedience* to their Refpective *Bifhops*. That the *Laity* fhou'd fubmit themfelves to the *Presbyters* and *Deacons*, as to the *Apoftolical College* under *Chrift*; and that the *Presbyters* and *Deacons*, as well as the *Laity*, fhou'd *Obey* their *Bifhop*, as *Chrift* Himfelf; whofe Perfon he did Reprefent: That therefore whoever kept not *Outward Communion* with his *Bifhop*, did forfeit his *Inward Communion* with *Chrift*: That no *Sacraments* were *Valid*, or *Acceptable* to *God*, which were not celebrated

brated in Communion with the *Bifhop*. That nothing in the *Church* fhou'd be done, nor any *Marriage* Contracted without the *Bifhop's* Confent, *&c.* As you will fee hereafter.

Thefe clear Teftimonies forc'd the*Presbyterians*(becaufe they were not in a Temper to be Convinc'd)to deny thefe *Epiftles* of St.*Ignatius* to be Genuine. But they have been fo fully Vindicated, particularly by the moft Learned Bifhop of *Chefter*, Dr. *Pearfon*,as to filence that Cavil, and leave no Pretence remaining againft *Epifcopacy* in that *Primitive* and *Apoftolical* Age.

S E C T. III.

Objection from the Times of Popery *in this Kingdom ; as if that did* Un-Church, *and confequently break the Succeffion of our* Bifhops.

I muft now Account for an Objection, which with fome, feems a mighty one, even enough to overthrow all that I have faid concerning the *Succeffion* of our *Bifhops* : And that is, the long *Mid-night* of *Popery*, which has, in old Time, Darken'd thefe Nations.

Well. The *Succeffion*, of which I have been fpeaking, was no Part of that Darknefs ; and we have, by God's Bleffing, recover'd our felves; in a great Meafure, from that Darknefs. But that Darknefs was fuch, as, with fome, to Deftroy the *Epifcopal Succeffion* becaufe, as they fay, fuch *great Errors*, efpecially that of *Idolatry*, does quite *Un-church* a People; and confequently muft break their *Succeffion*.

I. This, by the way, is a *Popifh* Argument, tho' they that now make it, are not aware of it. For the Church of *Rome* argues thus, That *Idolatry* does *Un-church*; and therefore, if fhe was *Idolatrous*, for fo long a time as we charge upon her, it will follow that, for fo many Ages, there was no *Vifible Church*, at leaft, in thefe *weftern* Parts of the World. And *Arianifm* (which is *Idolatry*) having broke in feveral times upon the *Church*; if *Idolatry* did quite *Un-church*, and Break the *Succeffion*, ther wou'd not be a *Chriftian Church* hardly left in the World. The Confequence

of

of which wou'd be as fatal to the *Church* of *Rome*, as to us : Therefore let her look to that Position, which she has advanced against us, that *Idolatry* does *Un-church*.

II. But that it does not *Un-church*, I have this to offer against those *Papists*, *Quakers*, and *Others* who make the Objection.

1. If it does quite *Un-church*, then cou'd no *Christian* be an *Idolater* ; because, by that, he wou'd, *ipso facto*, cease to be a Member of the *Christian Church* : But the *Scripture* does suppose that a *Christian* may be an *Idolater* : Therefore *Idolatry* does not *Un-church*. The *Minor* is prov'd, 1 *Cor.* v. 11. *If any Man that is called a Brother* (that is, a *Christian*) *be a Fornicator, or Covetous, or an Idolater*——Nay, *Eph.* v. 5. *a covetous man* is call'd an *Idolater* ; and *Col.* iii. 5. *Covetousness* is *Idolatry*. So that, by this Argument, *Covetousness* does *Un-church*. If it be said, that *Covetousness* is call'd *Idolatry*, only by Allusion, but that it is not *Formal* Idolatry : I know no Ground for that Distinction. The *Scripture* calls it *Idolatry*, and makes no Distinction. But,

2dly, In the first Text quoted, 1 *Cor.* v. 11. both *Covetousness* and *Idolatry* are Nam'd ; so that, you have both *Material* and *Formal*, or what other sort of *Idolatry* you please to fansie.

I grant, that, in one sense, *Idolatry* does *Un-church* ; that is, while we continue in it, it renders us Obnoxious to the *Wrath* of *God* ; and forfeits our Title to the *Promises* which are made to the *Church* in the *Gospel* : But, so does *Fornication, Covetousness*, and every other *Sin*, till we *Repent*, and *Return* from it. But none of these *Sins* do so *Un-church* us, as to Exclude our Returning to the *Fold*, by sincere Repentance ; or to need a second *Baptism*, or *Admission* into the *Church* : Neither does *Idolatry*. Do I then put *Idolatry* upon the level with other common *Sins* ? No, far from it. Every *Scab* is not a *Leprosie* ; yet a *Leper* is a *Man*, and may Recover his Health. *Idolatry* is a fearful *Leprosie* ; but it does not therefore quite *Un-church*, nor throw us out of the *Covenant*. For, if it did, then wou'd not *Repentance* heal it ; because *Repentance* is a great Part of the *Covenant*. And therefore, since none deny *Repentance* to an *Idolater* ; it follows that he is not yet quite out of the *Covenant*. Some of the *Ancients* have deny'd Repentance to *Apostacy*, yet granted it to *Idolatry* ; which shews that they did not look upon *Idolatry* to be an absolute *Apostacy* ; for every *Sin* is an *Apostacy*, in a Limited sense.

2. Let

2. Let us, in this Diſquiſition, follow the Example before mention'd, of the *Apoſtles* and *moſt Primitive Fathers*, to meaſure the
Chriſtian Church with its exact *Type*, the Church under the *Law*;
which are not *Two Churches*, but Two *States* of the ſame *Church*, for
it is the ſame *Chriſtian* Church, from the firſt Promiſe of *Chriſt*,
Gen. iii. 15. to the End of the World. And therefore it is ſaid,
Heb. iv. 2. That the *Goſpel* was Preached unto *Them*, as well as
unto *Us*. And theſe two *States* of the Church, *before* and *after*
Chriſt, do Anſwer, like a pair of *Indentures* to one another; the
one being, to an *Iota* fulfilled in the other.   *Matth.* v. 18.

Now we find frequent Lapſes to *Idolatry* in the *Church*
of the *Jews*: Yet did not this *Un-church* them; no, nor deprive them
of a competent meaſure of God's Holy Spirit; as it is written, *Neh.*
ix. 18, 20. *Yea, when they had made them a molten calf, and ſaid, this
is thy God——yet thou, in thy manifold Mercies, forſookeſt them not
——Thou gaveſt thy good ſpirit to inſtruct them,* &c.

And let it be here obſerv'd, That tho' God ſent many *Prophets*
to Reprove the great *wickedneſs* and *Idolatry*, as well of their *Prieſts*
as *People*; yet none of theſe *Holy Prophets* did ſeparate Communion from the *wicked Prieſts*: They wou'd not joyn in their *Idolatrous*
Worſhip; but in all other Parts, they joyn'd with them; and
ſet up no oppoſit *Prieſthood* to them. So little did the *Prophets* think
that their *Idolatry* had either *Un-church'd* them, or broke the *Succeſſion* of their *Prieſts*; or that it was Lawful for any, how *Holy*
ſoever, to uſurp upon their *Prieſthood*, and ſupply the Deficiencies
of it to the *People*. And apply to this, what I have before ſhewn,
in the words of St. *Clement*; whoſe *Name is written in the Book of
Life*, That the *Evangelical Prieſthood*, is as ſurely fixed, in the *Biſhops* of the *Church*, and its *Succeſſion* continu'd in thoſe *Ordain'd*
by them, as the *Levitical Prieſthood* was confirm'd by the Budding
of *Aaron*'s *Rod*, and to be continu'd in that *Tribe*.

III. And here let our *Korahites*, of ſeveral ſizes, take a view of
the Heinouſneſs of their *Schiſm*; and let them not think their
Crime to be nothing, becauſe they have been taught, with their
Nurſes Milk, to have the utmoſt abhorrence to the very Name
of a *Biſhop*; tho' they cou'd not tell why. Let them rather conſider ſeriouſly the misfortune of their Education, which ſhou'd
make them Strangers, to all the reſt of the Chriſtian World but

them-

themſelves in a Corner ; and to all the former Ages of *Chriſti-anity.*

They have been told that *Epiſcopacy* is *Popery*; becauſe the *Papiſts* have *Biſhops.*

So have they *Presbyters* too, that is, *Pariſh Prieſts* : They have the *Creed* likewiſe, and the Holy *Scriptures* ; and all theſe muſt be *Popiſh,* if this be a good *Argument.*

But, are they willing to be undeceived ? Then they muſt know that *Epiſcopacy* has none ſo great an Enemy as the *Papacy* ; which wou'd Engroſs the whole *Epiſcopal* Power, into the ſingle *See* of *Rome* ; by making all other *Biſhops* abſolutly dependent upon that, which only they call the *Apoſtolical* Chair. And no longer ſince than the *Council* of *Trent*, the *Pope* endeavor'd, with all his Intereſt, to have *Epiſcopacy*, except only that of the *Biſhop* of *Rome,* to be declar'd not to be *Jure Divino*. By which non other *Biſhops* cou'd claim any other Power, but what they had from Him. But that *Council* was not ſo quite Degenerated as to ſuffer this to paſs.

And the *Jeſuits*, and Others, who Diſputed there on the *Pope's* part, us'd thoſe ſame Arguments againſt the *Divine Right* of *Epiſcopacy*, which from them, and the *Popiſh Canoniſts* and *Schoolmen* have been lick'd up by the *Presbyterians* and others of our *Diſſenters.* They are the ſame Arguments which are us'd by *Pope* and *Presbyter* againſt *Epiſcopacy.*

When the *Pope* cou'd not carry his Cauſe againſt *Epiſcopacy* in the Council of *Trent*, he took another Method, and that was, to ſet up a vaſt Number of *Presbyterian* Prieſts, that is, the *Regulars*, whom he Exempted from the *Juriſdiction* of their reſpective *Biſhops*, and fram'd them into a *Method* and *Diſcipline* of their own, accountable only to *Superiors* of his, and their own contriving ; which is exactly the *Presbyterian* Model.

Theſe *Uſurpations* upon the *Epiſcopal* Authority, made the Famous Archbiſhop of *Spalato*, quit his great Preferments in the *Church* of *Rome*, and Travel into *England*, in the Reign of King *James* I. to ſeek for a more *Primitive* and *Independent Epiſcopacy.* Himſelf, in his *Conſilium Profectionis*, gives theſe ſame Reaſons for it : And that this ſhameful *Depreſſion* and *Proſtitution* of *Epiſcopacy*, in the *Church* of *Rome*, was the cauſe of his leaving her.

He

He obſerv'd truly, that the further we ſearch upward in *Anti-quity*, there is ſtill more to be found of the *Epiſcopal*, and leſs of the *Papal* Eminency.

St. *Ignatius* is full, in every line almoſt, of the high Authority of the *Biſhop*, next and immediately under *Chriſt*; as all the other Writers in thoſe Primitive Times: But there is a profound ſilence in them all of that *Supremacy* in the *Biſhop* of *Rome*, which is now claim'd over all the other *Biſhops* of the *Catholick Church*: Which cou'd not be, if it had been then known in the World. This had been a ſhort and effectual Method, whereby St. *Paul*, or St. *Clement* might have quieted the great *Schiſm* of the *Corinthi-ans*, againſt which they both wrote, in their *Epiſtles* to them; to bid them refer their Differences to the *Infallible Judge* of *Contro-verſy*, the *Supreme Paſtor* at *Rome*. But not a word like this. Eſpe-cially conſidering that St. *Peter* was one, for whom ſome of theſe *Corinthians* ſtrove (1 Cor. i. 12.) againſt thoſe who preferred others before Him.

The *Uſurp'd Supremacy* of the later *Biſhops* of *Rome* over their *Fel-low-Biſhops*, has been as Fatal to *Epiſcopacy*, as the Rebellion of our yet later *Presbyters* againſt their Reſpective *Biſhops*.

And indeed, whoever wou'd write the true Hiſtory of *Presbyte-rianiſm*, muſt begin at *Rome*, and not at *Geneva*.

So very *Groundleſs*, as well as *Malicious*, is that popular Cla-mour of *Epiſcopacy* having any Relation to *Popery*. They are ſo utterly Irreconcilable, that it is impoſſible they can ſtand toge-ther: For that moment that *Epiſcopacy* were Reſtor'd to its Pri-mitive Independency, the *Papacy*, that is, that *Supremacy*, which does now diſtinguiſh it, muſt *ipſo facto* ceaſe. But enough of this, for I muſt not digreſs into various Subjects.

I have ſhewn, in Anſwer to the Objection of the Ages of *Pope-ry* in this Kingdom, that all thoſe *Errors*, even *Idolatry* it ſelf, does not *Un-church*, nor break *Succeſſion*. And 2dly, I have Exem-plifi'd this from the Parallel of the *Jewiſh Church*, under the *Law*. Then applying of this to our Caſe, I have vindicated *Epiſcopacy* from the Imputation of *Popery*. I will now go on to further *Rea-ſons*, why the *Succeſſion* of our preſent *Biſhops* is not hurt by that Deluge of *Popery*, which once cover'd the face of this Land.

IV. The end of all *Government*, as well in the *Church* as *State*, is to preſerve *Peace*, *Unity*, and *Order*; and this cannot be done, if the *Mis-adminiſtration* of the *Officers* in the Government, did *Vacate* their *Commiſſion*, without its being Re-call'd by thoſe who gave ſuch *Commiſſion* to them. For then, 1ſt. Every Man muſt be Judge, when ſuch a *Commiſſion* is *Vacated*; and then no Man is bound to obey longer than he pleaſes. 2*dly*; One may ſay it is *Vacated*, another not; whence perpetual Contention muſt ariſe.

A Man may *Forfeit* his Commiſſion, that is, do thoſe things, which give juſt Cauſe to his *Superiors* to take it from him: But it is not actually *Vacated*, till it be actually *Recall'd* by thoſe who have lawful Power to take it from him: Otherwiſe their cou'd be no *Peace* nor *Certainty* in the World, either in *Publick* or in *Private* affairs. No *Family* cou'd ſubſiſt. No Man enjoy an *Eſtate*. No *Society* whatever cou'd keep together: And the *Church* being an *Outward Society* (as ſhewn in the *Diſcourſe* of *Water Baptiſm*) muſt conſequently ſubſiſt by thoſe *Laws* which are indiſpenſible to every *Society*. And tho' *Idolatry* does juſtly *Forfeit* the *Commiſſion* of any *Church*, in this ſenſe, that God's Promiſes to Her being *Conditional*, He may juſtly take her *Commiſſion* from her, and *Remove* her *Candleſtick* : Now tho' her *Commiſſion* be thus *Forfeitable*, yet it ſtill *Continues*, and is not actually *Vacated*, till God ſhall pleaſe *actually* to Recall it, or take it away: For no *Commiſſion* is *Void*, till it be ſo *Declar'd*. Thus, tho' the *Jews* did often fall into *Idolatry*, yet (as before has been ſaid) God did bear long with them; and did not *Un-church* them, tho' they had juſtly *Forfeited*. And theſe wicked *Husband men*, who ſlew thoſe whom the *Lord* ſent for the Fruits of His *Vineyard*, yet continu'd ſtill to be the *Husband-men* of the *Vineyard*, till their *Lord* did Diſpoſſeſs them, and gave their *Vineyard* unto others.

And *natural Reaſon* does enforce this: If a *Steward* abuſe his Truſt, and oppreſſes the *Tenants*, yet are they ſtill oblig'd to pay their *Rent* to him, and his *Diſcharges* are ſufficient to them againſt their *Landlord*, till he ſhall *Superſede* ſuch a *Steward*.

If a *Captain* wrong and cheat his *Soldiers*, yet are they oblig'd to remain under his Command, till the *King*, who gave him his *Commiſſion*, or thoſe to whom he has Committed ſuch an Authority, ſhall *Caſhier* him.

And thus it is in the *Sacerdotal Commiſſion*, Abuſes in it, do not take it away, till God, or thoſe to whom He has Committed ſuch an an Authority, ſhall *Suſpend, Deprive,* or *Degrade* (as the *Fact* Requires) ſuch a *Biſhop* or a *Prieſt.*

And there is this higher Conſideration in the *Sacerdotal Commiſſion,* than in thoſe of Civil Societies; That it being immediately from *God,* as *none* (therefore) *can take this Honour to himſelf, but he that is called of God, as was* Aaron; ſo can none take it away, but he that is as *Expreſly* and *Outwardly* called thereunto, as *Aaron* was to be a *Prieſt.* For this wou'd be to Uſurp upon *God's* immediate *Prerogative,* which is to Conſtitute His own *Prieſts.* Upon this Foundation I argue.

V. As the *neceſſity* of *Government,* and the general Commands in *Scripture,* of *Obedience* to *Government* do require our Submiſſion to the Government in being, where there is no *Competition* concerning the *Titles,* or any that *Claims* a *better Right* than the *Poſſeſſor:* So where a *Church,* once Eſtabliſh'd by *God,* tho' ſuffering many Interruptions, does continue, Her *Governors* ought to be acknowledg'd; where ther is no *better Claim* ſet up againſt them.

This was the Reaſon why our *Saviour* and His *Apoſtles* did, without ſcruple, acknowledge the *High-Prieſt* and *Sanhedrin* of the *Jews* in their time; tho' from the days of the *Maccabees,* ther had been great *Irruptions,* and *Breaches* in the due *Succeſſion* of their *Prieſts:* and before *Chriſt* came, and all His time, the *Romans,* as *Conquerors,* diſpos'd of the *Prieſthood* as they pleas'd; and made it *Annual* and *Arbitrary,* which *God* had appointed *Hereditary* and *Unmovable.*

But ther was then no *Competition:* The *Jews* did ſubmit to it, becauſe they were under the ſubjection of the *Romans,* and cou'd have no other. No *High-Prieſt* claimed againſt him in Poſſeſſion, but all ſubmitted to him.

And our *Saviour* did confirm His Authority, and of the *Sanhedrin,* or Inferior *Prieſts* with him, *(Matth.* xxiii. 2.) ſaying, *the Scribes and Phariſees ſit in Moſes's ſeat. All therefore, whatſoever they bid you obſerve, that obſerve and do.* And St. *Paul* own'd the Authority of the *High-Prieſt, Act.* xxiii. 5.

Many Objections might have been rais'd againſt the Deduction of their *Succeſſion* from *Moſes:* But ther being none who claim'd any better Right than they had; therefore their *Right* was Uncontroverted; and by our *Saviour's* Authority was Confirm'd.

Now

Now suppose some *Interruptions* had been in the *Succession,* or *Corruptions* in the *Doctrine* and *Worship* of our *English Bishops,* in former Ages, yet (as in the Case of the *Scribes* and *Pharisees*) that cou'd have no Effect to Invalidate their *Commission* and *Authority* at the present.

SECT. IV.

The Assurance *and* Consent *in the* Episcopal Communion, *beyond that of any other.*

I. THE whole *Christian* World, as it always has been, so at this Present, it is *Episcopal;* except a few *Dissenters,* who, in less than Two Hundred years last past, have arisen, like a *wart* upon the Face of the *western* Church. For little more Proportion do our *Dissenters* here, the *Hugonots* in *France,* the *Presbyterians* in *Holland, Geneva,* and thereabouts, bear to the whole Body of the *Latin* Church, which is all *Episcopal.* But, if you compare them with the *Catholick* Church all over the World, which is all *Episcopal,* they will not appear so big as a *Mole.*

II. If our *Dissenters* think it much, that the Church of *Rome* shou'd be reckon'd in the List against them; we will be content to leave them out: Nay more, if we shou'd give them all those *Churches,* which own the *Supremacy* of *Rome* to be joyn'd with them (as they are the nearest to them) it will be so far from casting the Ballance on their side, that the other *Episcopal* Churches will, by far, out-number them both.

Let us then, to these *Dissenters* against *Episcopacy,* add the *Churches* of *Italy,* and *Spain* entire, with the *Popish* Part of *Germany, France, Poland* and *Hungary* (I think they have no more to reckon upon,) against these we produce the vast *Empire* of *Russia* (which is greater in Extent than all these *Popish* Countries before nam'd) *England, Scotland, Denmark, Sweden,* and all the *Lutheran* Churches in *Germany;* which will out-number both the *Papists* and *Presbyterians* before-mention'd. And this comparison is only made as to the *Latin* Church. But then, we have all the rest of the *Christian* World, wholly on the *Episcopal* side, against both the *Supre-*

macy

macy of *Rome*, and P*arity* of the *Presbyterians*. The whole *Greek*
Church, the *Armenians*, *Georgians*, *Mingrelians*, *Jacobites*, the
Chriſtians of St. *Thomas*, and St. *John* in the *Eaſt-Indies*, and o-
ther *Oriental* Churches. Then in *Africa*, the *Cophties* in *Egypt*,
and great Empire of the *Abyſſins* in *Æthiopia*. Theſe all are *Epiſ-*
copal, and never own'd the *Supremacy* of *Rome*: And over reckon,
out of ſight, all that diſown *Epiſcopacy*, and all that own the *Su-*
premacy of *Rome* with them.

III. Let me add, that among our *Diſſenters*, every Claſs of
them does Condemn all the reſt; the *Presbyterian* Damns the
Quaker, the *Quaker* Damns him, *Independent*, *Baptiſt*, &c. All
Damn one another, and Each denys the others *Ordination* or
Call.

So that, the *Ordination* of every one of them, is diſown'd by
all the reſt; and all of them together by the whole *Chriſtian* World.
And if their *Ordinations* are not Valid, then they have no more Authority to adminiſter the *Sacraments*, than any other *Lay-men*;
and conſequently, ther can be no ſecurity in Receiving *Baptiſm*
from any of them.

IV. What allowances God will make to thoſe who think
their *Ordination* to be good enough, and that they are true *Mi-*
niſters of the *Goſpel*; and, as ſuch, do receive the *Sacraments* from
them, I will not determine.

But they have no reaſon to expect the like allowances who are
warned of it before-hand, and will notwithſtanding venture upon
it; before theſe *Diſſenters* have *fully* and *clearly* acquit themſelves
of ſo *Great* and *Univerſal* a Charge laid againſt them; ſuch an
one, as muſt make the whole *Chriſtian* World *wrong*, if they be
in the *Right*! Not only the preſent *Chriſtian Churches*, but all the
Ages of *Chriſtianity* ſince *Chriſt*. Of which the *Diſſenters* are deſir'd to produce any one, in any Part of the World, that were
not *Epiſcopal*——any one Conſtituted *Church* upon the Face of the
Earth, that was not Govern'd by *Biſhops*, diſtinct from, and Superior to *Presbyters*, before the *Vaudois* in *Piedmont*, the *Hugonots*
in *France*, the *Calviniſts* in *Geneva*, and the *Presbyterians* thence
Tranſplanted, in this laſt Age, into *Holland*, *Scotland* and *England*.

V. If it ſhou'd be retorted, that neither is the *Church of Eng-*
land without *Oppoſers*; for, that the *Church* of *Rome* oppoſes Her,
as do likewiſe our *Diſſenters*.

E   *Anſ.*

Anf. None of them do oppofe Her, in the Point we are now upon, that is, the Validity of *Epifcopal* Ordination, which the *Church* of *Rome* does own; and the *Presbyterians* dare not deny it, becaufe they wou'd (thereby) overthrow all their own *Ordinations*; for the *Presbyters* who *Reformed* (as they call it) from *Bifhops*, receiv'd their *Ordination* from *Bifhops*.

And therefore, tho' the *Epifcopal* Principles do *Invalidate* the *Ordination* by *Presbyters*, yet the *Presbyterian* Principles do not *Invalidate* the *Ordination* by *Bifhops*: So that the *Validity* of *Epifcopal* *Ordination* ftands fafe, on all fides, even by the Confeffion of thofe who are Enemies to the *Epifcopal Order*: and, in this, the *Bifhops* have no oppofers.

Whereas, on the other hand, the *Validity* of the *Presbyterian* *Ordinations*, is own'd by none but themfelves; and they have all the reft of the World as oppofite to them.

Therefore, to ftate the Cafe the moft Impartially, to receive *Baptifm* from thefe *Diffenters*, is, at leaft, a *hazard* of many Thoufands to One; as many as all the reft of *Chriftianity* are more than they: But to receive it from the *Bifhops*, or *Epifcopal* Clergy, has no *hazard* at all, as to its *Validity*, even as own'd by the *Presbyterians* themfelves.

SECT. V.

The Perfonal Sanctity *of the Adminiftrator of the Sacraments, tho' highly Requifite on his Part, yet not of Neceffity as to the Receivers, to Convey to them the Benefits of the Sacraments.*

I. THE only Objection of thofe *Quakers*, who are otherwife convinc'd of the *Obligation* of the *Sacraments*, is the *Neceffity* they think ther is of great *Perfonal* Holinefs in the *Adminiftrators*; without which, they cannot fee how the *Spiritual* Effects of the *Sacraments* can be convey'd. But I wou'd befeech them to confider, how, by this, inftead of referring the Glory to *God*, and *leffening* the *Performance* of *Man*, which I charitably

pre-

presume (and I am confident as to some of whom I speak) that
it is their true and sincere Intention; but instead of that, I do,
in great Good-will, invite them to reflect whither their well-in-
tended Zeal has turn'd the Point of this Question——even to o-
ver-magnifie *Man*, and transfer the Glory of *God* unto His *weak
Instrument*; as if any (the least Part) of the *Divine* Vertue which
God has annexed to His *Sacraments* did proceed from His *Minister*. If this be not the meaning (as sure it is not) why so much
stress laid upon the *Sanctity* of the *Ministers*? as if thro'
their power or holiness the *Holy Ghost* was given? Act. iii. 12.

II. To obviate this pretence, our Saviour *Christ* chose a *Devil*
(*John* vi. 70.) to be one of His *Apostles*; and he was sent to *Baptize*
and work *Miracles* as well as the rest: And those whom *Judas*
did *Baptize*, were, no doubt, as well *Baptized*, and did partake
of the Communication of the *Spirit* (according to their Preparation for it) as much as any who were *Baptized* by the other *Apostles*; unless you will say that *Christ* sent him to *Baptize*, who had
no Authority to *Baptize*, and that none shou'd receive Benefit by
his *Baptism*, which wou'd be to Cheat and Delude the People;
and is a great Blasphemy against *Christ*, and a distrust of His *Power*;
as if it were *Limited* by the poor Instrument He pleases to make
use off; whereas,

III. His *Greatness* is often most *Magnify'd* in the *meaness* of the
Instruments, by which He works. Thus He destroy'd *Egypt* by *Frogs*
and *Lice*; and the *Philistines* by *Emerods* and *Mice*; and sent
His *Armies* of *Flies* and *Hornets* to dispossess the *Canaanites*. *Out
of the mouths of babes and sucklings hast thou ordained
strength, because of thine enemies, that thou mightest* Psal. viii. 2.
still the enemy; and the avenger; i. e. That the Enemies of God
might be confounded, when they saw His great Power Exerted
by such weak and contemptible *Instruments*. The Walls of *Je-
richo* (the *Type* of *Spiritual* wickedness) were thrown down by
the blast of seven *Rams Horns*, when blown by the *Priests* whom
He had commanded: And He rebuked the Iniquity of *Balaam*
by the mouth of an *Ass*, to shew that no *Instruments* are *Ineffectual*
in His Hands; and made use of the mouth of *Balaam* to Prophesie
of *Christ*. For this cause, says St. *Barnabas*, in
his *Catholick Epistle*, c. 5. did *Christ* choose Men   ὑπὲρ πᾶσ' ἁμαρ-
who were *Exceeding great Sinners* to be His *A-*   τίαν ἀνομωτέρους.

postles;

poftles ; to fhew the Greatnefs of His *Power* and *Grace* ; and put the Ineftimable *Treafure* of His *Gofpel* into *Earthen Veffels*, that the Praife might be to *God*, and not to Men.

Phil. i. 16. IV. St. *Paul* rejoyced in *Chrift* being Preached, tho' not *fincerely* by thofe who did it ; becaufe God can bring *Good* out of *Evil* ; and by wicked *Inftruments*, Propagate His *Gofpel* ; turning their *malice* (even of the *Devil* himfelf) to the furtherance of the *Faith*: Otherwife the *Apoftle* cou'd have no caufe to *Rejoyce* in the Preaching of *wicked* Men, if none cou'd receive benefit by it. And he plainly fuppofes, 1 *Cor.* ix. 27. That a Man may fave others by his *Preaching*, and yet himfelf be a *caft-away*.

V. And fo far as we can know or judge any thing, we fee daily Experience of this ; That God has touched Mens Hearts upon hearing the *Truth* fpoken, tho' by Men who were great *Hypocrites*, and very *wicked*. And what reafon can be given to the contrary ? *Truth* is *Truth* whoever fpeaks it : And if my Heart be prepared, the *good Seed* receives no evil *Tincture* of the Hand that fowed it : And who can Limit *God*, that His *Grace* may not go along with me in this ?

I have heard fome of the *now feparate Quakers* confefs, that they have formerly felt very fenfible Operations of the *Spirit*, upon the *Preaching* of fome of thofe whom they have fince Detected of *grofs Errors* and *Hypocrifies* ; and they now think it ftrange. But this were enough to convince them, that *the wind bloweth where it lifteth* : otherwife they muft condemn themfelves, and confefs that, in all that time, they had no true Participation of the *Spirit* of God, but that what they miftook for it, was a meer *Delufion* : Or elfe confefs that by the *Truths* which were fpoken by thefe *Minifters* of *Satan* (for they fpeak fome Truths) God might work a good Effect upon the Hearts of fome *well-difpos'd*, tho' then *Ignorant*, and much *Deluded* People. If not fo, we muft judge very feverely of all thofe who live in *Idolatrous* or *Schifmatical* Countries ; ther were *great Prophets* and *good Men* among the *Ten Tribes*. And if the *words*, nay *Miracles*, of *Chrift*, did render the Hearts of many yet more obdurate, even to fin againft the *Holy Ghoft* ; which was the reafon why He fometimes refus'd to work *Miracles* among them, becaufe thereby they grew worfe and worfe ; and if the Preaching of the *Gofpel*, by the mouths of *Apoftles*, became the favour of *Death*, to *wicked*

Matth. xii. from v. 2 . to v. 32.

and

and *unprepar'd* Hearts; why may not the words of *Truth* have a good Effect upon *honeſt* and *good* Minds, tho' ſpoken from the mouth of an *Hypocrite*, or of Perſons, who, in other things, are greatly *Deluded*?

I have before mention'd the *Wizard* Major *Weir*, who *Bewitched* the *Presbyterians* in *Scotland*, ſince the *Reſtoration*, 1660, as much as *Simon Magus* did the *Samaritans*: And yet I ſuppoſe the more moderate of the *Quakers* will not raſhly give all over to Deſtruction, who blindly followed him, and admir'd his *Gifts*; or will ſay but that ſome words of Truth he might drop, might have a real good Effect upon ſome *well-meaning*, tho' groſly *Deluded* People, who followed him. Two of *Winder's witches* (ſee *The Snake in the Graſs*, p. 300. 2*d*. Edit.) were *Preachers* among the *Quakers* for Twenty years together; and thought to be as *Powerful* and *Affecting* as any others.

VI. But, the Argument will hold ſtronger againſt them, as to the *Sacraments*, than in the Office of *Preaching*; becauſe in *Preaching* much depends upon the Qualifications of the Perſon, as to *Invention*, *Memory*, *Judgment*, &c. But in the Adminiſtration of an *Outward Sacrament*, nothing is requir'd, as of *Neceſſity*, but the lawfulneſs of the *Commiſſion*, by which ſuch a Perſon does Adminiſter; and a ſmall meaſure of *natural* or *acquir'd* Parts is ſufficient to the *Adminiſtration*.

Therefore let us lay no ſtreſs upon the *Inſtrument* (more than was upon the *waters* of *Jordan* to heal *Naaman*) but truſt wholly upon the *Commiſſion*, which conveys the *Vertue* from *God*, and not from His *Miniſters*: That all the *Glory* may be to *God*, and not to *Man*.

'Tis true, the *Perſonal* Qualifications of the *Inſtrument* are *Lovely* and *Deſirable*; but they become a *Snare*, where we expect any part of the *Succeſs* from them. This was the ground of the *Corinthian* Schiſm (1 *Cor.* i. 11.) and, tho' unſeen, of ours at this Day.

VII. And the conſequences of it, are of manifold and fatal Deſtruction.

1. This unſettles all the *Aſſurance* we can have in God's *Promiſe* to aſſiſt His own *Inſtitution*; for, if the *Vertue*, or any part of it, lies in the *Holineſs* of the *Inſtrument*, we can never be ſure of the Effect;

Effect, as to us; because, we have no *certain* knowledge of the *Holiness* of another. *Hypocrites* deceive even *good Men*.

2. This wou'd quite disappoint the *Promise* Christ has made, *Matth.* xxviii. 20. To be with His *Ministers*, in the Execution of His Commission, to *Baptize*, &c. *always, even unto the end of the world*. For, if the *Holiness* of the *Instrument* be a *necessary* Qualification, this may fail, nay always must fail, so far as we can be *sure* of it; and consequently *Christ* has commanded *Baptism* and *His Supper* to continue, *to the end of the world*, till *his coming again*; and yet has not afforded *means* whereby they may be continu'd; which He has not done, if the *Holiness* of the *Administrator* be a *necessary* Qualification, and that He has not left us a *certain* Rule, whereby to judge of the *Holiness* of another: And thus have you rendred the *Command* of *Christ* of none Effect, thro' your Tradition.

3. This is contrary to all God's former Institutions. The *wickedness* of the *Priests*, under the *Law*, did not *excuse* any of the People from bringing of their *Sacrifices* to the *Priests*: The *Priests* were to Answer for their own Sin, but the *People* were not answerable for it, or their *Offerings* the less accepted.

But we were in a much worse condition, under the *Gospel-Administration*, if the Effect of *Christ*'s Institutions, did depend either *wholly*, or in *part* upon the *Personal Holiness* of His *Priests*. This wou'd put us much more in their Power, than it is the Intention of those who make this objection to allow to them: This magnifies *Men*, more than is due to them; therefore I will apply the Apostle's words to this Case; *Let no man glory in men; who is Paul? and who is Apollo? but ministers—so then, neither is he that planteth any thing, neither he that watereth; but God who giveth the increase.* 1 Cor. iii. 21.

4. This was (with others) the Error of the Ancient *Donatists*; those Proud and Turbulent *Schismaticks*, the great *Disturbers* of the *Peace* of the Church, upon an opinion of their own *Sanctity*, above that of other Men: For which reason, they rejected all *Baptisms*, except what was performed by themselves; and *Re-baptiz'd* those who came over to them, from the *Church*; for, they said that the *Holiness* of the *Administrator* was *necessary* towards conveying the *Spiritual Graces* of *Baptism*: Thus they argu'd; *Qui non habet quod Det, quomodo Dat?* i. e. How shall a Man give that

to another; which he has not himself? But *Optatus* Answers them, that *God* was the *Giver*, and not *Man*, *Videte Deum esse Datorem*. And he argues that it was preferring *Themselves* before *God*, to think that the *Vertue* of *Baptism* did come from *Them*; that they were nothing but *Ministers* or *Work-men*; and that, as when a *Cloth* was *Dyed*, the change of the *Cloth* came from the *Colours* infus'd, not from the vertue of the *Dyer*. So that in *Baptism* the *Change* of the *Baptized*, came from the *Vertue* of the *Sacrament*; not from the *Administrator*: That it was the *Water* of *Baptism*, which did *wash*, not the Person who apply'd the *Water*. That the *Personal Sanctity* of the *Administrator* signify'd nothing to the *Efficacy* of the *Sacrament*: Therefore, says he, *Nos operemur, ut Ille det, qui se daturum esse promisit*, i. e. Let us work, that God, who has promis'd it, may bestow the Effect: And that when we work, *Humana sunt opera, sed Dei sunt Munera*, i. e. The *Work* is *Man's*, but the *Gift* is *God's*. And thence he exposes that *Jam illud quam Ridiculum est*, Ridiculous Principle of the *Donatists*, *quod, quasi ad Gloriam vestram*, which they advanc'd to *à vobis semper auditur, hoc munus* gain *Glory* to *Themselves*; that *Baptismatis, est Dantis, non Accipientis?* p. 89. the *Gift* in *Baptism* was of the *Administrator*, and not of the *Receiver*: But he shews, that the *Gift* was conferred by *God*, proportionably to the *Faith* of the *Receiver*, and not according to the *Holiness* of the *Administrator*.

The *Discourse* is large, to which I refer the *Reader*. I have given this *Tast* of it, to let these see to whom I now write, that they have (tho' unaware) stumbled upon the very *Notion* of the *Donatists*, which divided them from the *Catholick Church*, and which, with them, has been long since Exploded by the whole *Christian* World; and I hope this may bring them to a more sober mind, to consider *from whence*, and *with whom* they have fallen; and to return again to the *Peace* of the *Church*, and the Participation of the Blessed *Sacraments* of *Christ*; and the Inestimable *Benefits* which He has promis'd to the *Worthy Receivers* of them.

Lastly, Let me observe that this *Error* of the *Donatists* and *Quakers*, borders near upon *Popery*; nay rather seems to exceed it. For the *Church* of *Modern Rome* makes the *Validity* of the *Sacraments* to depend upon the *Intention* of the *Priest*; but his *Intention* is much more in his own Power; and there are more evident *Signs* of it than of his *Holiness*. VIII. I

Adv. Parmen. l. 5. de schismat. Donatist. Ed. Paris 1631. p 87

p. 88.

VIII. I wou'd not have the *Quakers* imagine that any thing I have said, was meant in excuse for the ill Lives of the *Clergy* of the *Church* of *England*; as if the *Diſſenters* were unblamable, but our *Clergy* wholly Proſtitute to all wickedneſs; and that for this cauſe, we plead againſt the *Sanctity* of the *Adminiſtrator*, as Eſſential to the *Sacrament*.

No, That is far from the Reaſon: I do not love to make compariſons, or Perſonal Reflections. If all Men be not as they ſhou'd be, pray God make them ſo. But I think ther is no modeſt *Diſſenter* will be offended, if I ſay, that ther are of our *Biſhops* and *Clergy*, Men, not only of *Learning*, and *moral Honeſty*, but of *Devotion*, and *ſpiritual Illumination*; and as much of the *Sobriety* of Religion; and can give as many *Signs* of it, Equally at leaſt (to ſpeak modeſtly) as any of our *Diſſenters*, of what Denomination ſoever.

IX. And I hope, that what I have ſaid will, at leaſt, hinder the *Succeſſion* of the *Biſhops* from the *Apoſtles*, to be any *Objection* againſt them. And they being poſſeſs'd moreover of all the other *Pretences* of our *Diſſenters*, the Ballance muſt needs lie on their ſide, and *ſecurity* can only be with them; becauſe ther is *doubt* in all the other *Schemes* of the *Diſſenters*, if what I have ſaid can amount but to a *Doubt*. If the want of *Succeſſion* and *outward Commiſſion*, upon which *Chriſt* and His *Apoſtles*, and the whole *Chriſtian Church*, in all Ages, till the laſt *Century*; and in all Places, even at this Day, except ſome *Corners* in the *Weſt*; and the *Moſaical* Inſtitution before them, did, by the Expreſs Command of God, lay ſo great a ſtreſs; if all this make but a *Doubt* (it is ſtrange that it ſhou'd, at leaſt, that it ſhou'd not) in the mind of any conſidering Perſons; then can they not, with *Security*, Communicate with any of our *Diſſenters*; becauſe, if he that *Eateth* and *Doubteth* is Damned, much more he that ſhall do ſo in *Religious* matters; wherein chiefly this Rule muſt ſtand, that *whatſoever is not of Faith is ſin*.

Rom. xiv. 23.

X. But now, to argue a little; ad *hominem*, ſuppoſe that the *Succeſſion* of our *Biſhops* were loſt; and ſuppoſe, what the *Quakers* and ſome others wou'd have, that the Thread being broke, we muſt caſt a new knot, and begin again, and make an Eſtabliſhment amongſt our ſelves, the beſt we can. Well When this is done, ought not that *Eſtabliſhment* to be preſerv'd? Ought every one to break in upon it, without juſt cauſe? Shou'd every one

one take upon him (or *her*), to *Preach*, or *Baptize*, contrary to the *Rules* Eſtabliſh'd? This, I think, no *Society* of Men will allow; For, the Members of a *Society* muſt be ſubject to the *Rules* of the *Society*, otherwiſe it is no *Society*: And the *Quakers* of *Grace-church-ſtreet* Communion have contended as Zealouſly for this compliance as any.

Now then, ſuppoſe that the conſcientious *Quakers* to whom I ſpeak, ſhou'd lay no ſtreſs at all upon the *Succeſſion* of our *Biſhops*; and conſider our *Conſtitution* no otherwiſe than of an *Eſtabliſhment* by agreement amongſt our ſelves; yet even ſo, by their own Confeſſion, while they can find no fault with our *Doctrine* or *worſhip*, they ought not to make a *Schiſm* in this *Conſtitution*, which they found *Eſtabliſhed*; and they ought to return to it; and if a new *Knot* was caſt upon the broken *Thread* of *Succeſſion*, at the *Reformation* from *Popery*, that *Knot* ought not to be un-loſed, without apparent and abſolute *Neceſſity*; leſt if we caſt new *Knots* every Day, we ſhall have no *Thread* left *un-knotted*; and expoſe our ſelves to the Deriſion of the common Adverſary.

XI. Conſider the grievous Sin of *Schiſm* and *Diviſion*; it is no leſs than the Rending of *Chriſt's Body*; and therefore *great Things* ought to be born, rather than run into it; even *all things*, except only that which is *apparently ſinful*; and that by the *Expreſs words* of *Scripture*; and not from our own Imaginations, tho' never ſo ſtrong. And tho' ther are ſome Imperfections in our *Reformation*, as to *Diſcipline*, and all the *High Places* are not yet taken away (the Lord, of His Mercy, quickly remove them) yet I will be bold to ſay, that in our *Doctrine*, *Worſhip*, and *Hierarchy*, nothing can be objected that is contrary to the *Rule* of *Holy Scripture*, or any thing Enjoyn'd, which is *There* Forbid to be done: And nothing leſs can warrant any *Schiſm* againſt our *Church*.

XII. Now, to come to a Concluſion, upon the whole matter. If you cannot get *Baptiſm* as you wou'd have it, take it as you can get it. If you cannot find Men of ſuch *Perſonal* Excellencies as the *Apoſtles*, take thoſe who have the ſame *Commiſſion* which they had, deriv'd down to them by regular *Ordination*; who *Reform'd* from *Popery*, and have been the *Eſtabliſhed Church* of this *Nation*, ever ſince: And moreover are as un-exceptionable, in their *Lives* and *Converſations*, as any others. Theſe are all the ſecurities you can have (without new *Miracles*) for Receiving the *Sacraments* from Proper hands. And therefore ther is no doubt but God will accept

F   of of your *Obedience* in Receiving them from such hands; much rather than your *Disobedience* of His Command to be *Baptized*, because you are not pleas'd with those whom His Providence has, at this Day, left in the Execution of His Commission to *Baptize*; as if the weakness of His *Minister* cou'd obstruct the Operations of His *Spirit*, in making good His part of the Covenant, which He has promised.

XIII. Ther is an Objection against *Baptism*, which is not worth an Answer; but that I wou'd condescend to the meanest, and leave nothing behind which might be a stumbling block to any.

I have heard it urg'd, that ther is no visible Effects seen by our *Baptisms*; that Men remain *wicked* and *loose* notwithstanding; and therefore some do conclude that ther is no vertue in *Baptism.*

Answ. To make this Argument of any force, it must be prov'd that *none* do receive any Benefit by it. For, if *some* do receive Benefit by it, and *others* do not, this must be charg'd upon the *Disposition* of the *Recipient*; according to the known Rule, that *whatsoever is receiv'd, is receiv'd according to the disposition of the Receiver.* Thus the same *Meat* is turn'd into *good Nourishment* in an *healthy*, and into *noxious Humors* in a *vitiated Stomach.* *Simon Magus* receiv'd no Benefit by his *Baptism*; and after the *Sop* the Devil entred into *Judas*; yet the other *Apostles* receiv'd great Benefit by it: To some it is the savour of *Life*, even the Communion of *Chrift's Body* and *Blood*; to others of *Condemnation*, who *discern not the Lord's Body* in it, but receive it as a common thing: Therefore we are commanded to *examine* our selves, to *prepare* our *Hearts* for the *worthy* Receiving of it.

1 Cor. x. 16. c. xi. 29.

v. 28.

But some say, as the *Jews* to *Chrift*, *shew us a sign*: They wou'd have some *Miraculous* Effects, immediately to appear. These are Ignorant of the Operations of the *Spirit*; and to these I say, in the words of *Chrift*, Joh. iii. 8. *The wind bloweth where it listeth, and thou hearest the sound thereof, but canst not tell whence it cometh or whither it goeth; so is every one that is born of the Spirit.* It works *silently*, but *powerfully*; and its *Progress*, like the *growing* of our *Bodies*, is not all at once, but by Degrees; whose *motion* is Imperceptible to humane Eyes.

The true use that is to be made of this *Objection*, that so few (and yet they are not *few* who) receive the Inestimable Benefits which are convey'd in the *Sacraments* of *Chrift's* Institution, is this,

To

To take the greater Care, and the more Earneſtly to beg the Aſſiſtance of God's *Grace*, to *fit* and *prepare* us, for the *worthy* Receiving of them; but by no means to negleⅆt them : For thoſe who *refuſed* to come to the *Supper* were Rejeⅆted, as well as he who came without a *Wedding.Garment.*

A SUPPLEMENT.

THE ſtreſs of this *Diſcourſe* being Founded upon *Epiſcopacy*, and long *Quotations* being improper in ſo ſhort a method of Argument as I have taken; to ſupply that Defeⅆt, and, at the ſame time, to make it eaſier to the Reader, I have added, by way of *Supplement*, a ſhort *Index* or *Collection* of *Authorities*, in the firſt 450 Years after *Chriſt*, for *Epiſcopacy*, with reſpeⅆt to the *Presbyterian* Pretences, of making a *Biſhop* all one with a *Presbyter*, at leaſt with one of their *Moderators* : And, in the next place, I have ſhewn the ſenſe of the *Reformation*, as to *Epiſcopacy*. Take them as follows.

Some Authorities for Epiſcopacy, *as* diſtinⅆt *from and* Superior *to* Presbytery, *taken out of the* Fathers *and* Councils, *in the firſt Four Hundred and Fifty Years after* Chriſt.

Anno Domini 70. St. *Clement* Biſhop of *Rome,* and *Martyr,* of whom mention is made *Phil.* iv. 3. in his 1ſt. *Epiſt.* to the *Corinthians*; N. 42. p. 89. of the Edition at *Oxford,* 1677.

The Apoſtles having Preached the Goſpel, thro' Regions and Cities, did Conſtitute the firſt Fruits of them, having prov'd them by the Spirit, to be *Biſhops* and *Deacons* of thoſe who ſhou'd	Κατὰ χώρας ἕν τε πόλεις κηρύσσοντες, καὶ θεύον τὰς Ἀπαρχὰς αὐτῶ, δοκιμάσαντες τῷ πνεύματι, εἰς Ἐπισκόπες καὶ Διακόνες τῶ μελλόντων πιστεύειν, καὶ ἕτε ἐ κηνῶς, ἐκ γὸ δὴ πολλῶν χρόνων ἐγέγραπτο

believe;

believe; and this, not as a new thing, for many Ages before it was written concerning *B ſhops* and *De.cons* ; for, thus ſaith the Scripture, in a certain place, *I will conſtitute their* Biſhops *in Righteouſneſs, and their* Deacons *in Faith.*

Iſa Lx 17.

περὶ Ἐπισκόπων ᾧ Διακόνων· ὅτως ᾷ᷉ πε λέγει ἡ γϱαφή; καταϛήσω τὲς Ἐπισκόπες αὐτῷ ἐν δικαιοσωύη, καὶ τὲς Διακόνες αὐτῷ ἐν πίϛι.

What wonder is it then, that thoſe who were Intruſted by God, in Chriſt, with this Commiſſion, ſhou'd Conſtitute thoſe before ſpoke of?

Καὶ τὶ θαυμασὸν, εἰ οἱ ἐν Χριϛῷ πιϛεύϳ῍εντες παϱὰ Θεῦ ἔϱγον τοιῦτο, κατέϛησϛ τὲς πϱοειϱημβύϛς;

ibid. n. 44. And the *Apoſtles* knew by the Lord *Jeſus Chriſt,* that Conteſts wou'd ariſe concerning the *Epiſcopal* Name (or Order) and for this Cauſe, having perfect fore-knowledge (of theſe things) they did Ordain thoſe whom we have mention'd before; and moreover, did Eſtabliſh the Conſtitution, that other approved Men ſhou'd ſucceed thoſe who Dy'd, in their Office and Miniſtry.

Καὶ οἱ Ἀπόϛολοι ἡμῶν ἔγνωϛ διὰ ᷉ Κυϱίꜯ ἡμῶν Ἰησῦ Χριϛῦ, ὅτι Ἔϱις ἔϛαι ὀπὶ ᷉ ὀνόμαῑ Ϙ. ᷉ Ἐπισκοπῆς. διὰ ταύτlω ᷉ν τὴν αἰτίαν, πϱόγνωσιν εἰληφόϛης τελείαν, κατέϛησϛ τὲς πϱοειϱημβύϛς, ᷇ μεταξὺ ἐπινομlω δεδώκασιν, ὅπως ἐὰν κοιμηθῶσιν, διαδέϛ῍ωνᾳ ἕτεϱι δεδοκιμασμβύοι ἄνδϱες, ᷉ λειτεϱγίαν αὐτῷ.

Therefore thoſe that were Conſtituted by Them, or afterwards by other approved Men, with the Conſent of all the Church, and have Adminiſtred to the Flock of Chriſt unblamably, with Humility and Quietneſs, without all ſtain of filth or naughtineſs; and have carry'd a good Report, of a long time, from all Men, I think cannot, without great Injuſtice, be turn'd out of their Office: For, it will be no ſmall ſin to us, if we thruſt thoſe from their Biſhopricks who have Holily and without Blame offer'd our Gifts (and Praiers to God.) Bleſſed are thoſe

Τὲς ᷉ν καταϛαϳ῍εντας ὑπ᾽ ἐκείνων, ἢ μεταξὺ ὑφ᾽ ἑτέϱων ἐλλογίμων ἀνδϱῶν, σωυδοκησάσης ᷉ Ἐκκλησίας πάσης, ᷇ λειτεϱγήσανῑας ἀμέμπϛως τῷ ποιμνίῳ ᷉ Χριϛῦ μⷮ ταπεινοφϱοσωύης, ἡσύχως ᷇ ἀβαναύσως, μεμαϱτυϱημβύϛς ᷉ πολλοῖς-χϱόνοις ὑπὸ πάντων, τέϲϛϛς ᷉ δικαίως νομίζομβϛ ἀποβάλεσθαι ᷉ λειτϛϱγίας. ἁμαϱτία γὸ ᷉ μικϱὰ ἡμῖν ἔϛαι, ἐὰν τὲς ἀμέμπϛως ᷇ ὁσίως πϱοσενέγκονῑας τὰ δῶϱα ᷉ Ἐπισκοπῆς ἀποβάλωμβϛ. Μακάϱιοι οἱ πϱοοδοιποϱήσανῑες πϱεσβύϛϛϱοι, οἵτινες ἔγκαϱπον ᷇ τελείαν ἔϲϛον ᷉ ἀνάλυσιν. ᷉ γὸ ἐυλαβᾶ᷉ϳᾳ μή τις αὐτὲς μεταϛήϛϳ ἀπὸ ᷉ ἰδϱυμβύꜯ αὐτοῖς τόπου. Ὁϱῶμβϛ γὰϱ ὅτι

Priests who are happily Dead, for they are not afraid of being Ejected out of the Places in which they are Constituted. For, I understand that you have Depriv'd some, from their Ministry, who behaved themselves un-re-provable amongst you.

Par. 40. To the *High-Priest* his proper Offices were appointed; the *Priests* had their proper Order, and the *Levites* their peculiar Services, or *Deaconships*; and the *Lay-men*, what was proper for *Lay-men*.

ἐνίας ὑμεῖς μετηνάγετε καλῶς πολιτδομμύως ἐκ. ἀμέμπτως αὐτοῖς τετιμημλύης λειτσρχίας.

Τῷ γὰς Ἀρχιερεῖ ἴδιαι λειτσρχίαι δεδομέναι εἰσί' ⁀ τοῖς Ἱερεῦσιν ἴδιος ὁ τόπ⁀ προστέτακ), ⁀ λευΐταις ἴδιαι διακονίαι ἐπίκειν', λαϊκὸς ἄνθρωπ⁀ τοῖς λαϊκοῖς προστάγμασιν δέδεϫ.

This, as before shewn, St. *Clement* apply'd to the Distribution of Orders in the *Christian* Church; *Bishops, Priests,* and *Deacons.* And the *Office* of the *Levites,* is here call'd by the Word Διακονίαι i. e. the Office of *Deacons.*

A.D.71. St. *Ignatius,* a Glorious *Martyr of Christ,* was Constituted, by the Apostles, *Bishop* of *Antioch,* and did thereby think that he succeeded them (as all other *Bishops* do) in their full *Apostolical* Office. Thence he salutes the Church of the *Trallians,* in the *Fulness* of the *Apostolical Character;* and in his Epistle he says to them,

Ἦν ⁀ ἀπαζόμμι ἐν τῷ πληρώματι, ἐν Ἀποστολικῷ χαρακτῆρι.

Be subject to your Bishop as to the Lord——

Τῷ Ἐπισκόπῳ ὑποτάσσεσθε ὡς τῷ Κυρίῳ.

And to the *Presbyters,* as to the *Apostles* of *Christ---* Likewise the *Deacons* also, being *Ministers* of the Mysteries of *Christ,* ought to please in all things---Without these ther is no *Church* of the Elect-He is without, who does any thing without the *Bishop,* and *Presbyters,* and *Deacons* ; and such an one is Defiled in his Conscience.

Καὶ τοῖς Πρεσβυτέροις, ὡς Ἀποστόλοις Ἰησοῦ Χριστοῦ— Δεῖ δὲ ⁀ τοῖς Διακόνους ὄντας μυστηρίων χριστοῦ Ἰησοῦ κατὰ πάντα τρόπον ἀρέσκειν——χωρὶς τούτων Ἐκκλησία ἐκλεκτὴ, οὐκ ἔστιν—— ὁ ἦ ἐκτὸς ὢν, οὗτος ἐστιν ὁ χωρὶς τοῦ Ἐπισκόπου, ⁀ τῶν Πρεσβυτέρων, καὶ τῶν Διακόνων ᐧ τι πράσσων· ὁ τοιοῦτ⁀ μεμίανται τῆ συνειδότι.

In his *Epist.* to the *Magnesians,* he tells them, That they ought not to despise their *Bishop* for his youth, but to pay him all manner

Καὶ ὑμῖν ᐧ πρέπει μὴ καταφρονεῖν τῆς ἡλικίας τοῦ Ἐπισκόπου, ἀλλὰ κατὰ γνώμην Θεοῦ πατρὸς πᾶσαν ἐντροπὴν αὐτῷ ἀπονέμειν καθὼς

of

of Reverence, according to the Commandment of God the Father. And as I know that your Holy *Presbyters* do————

Therefore, as *Christ* did nothing without the *Father*, so neither do ye, whether *Presbyter*, *Deacon*, or *Laick*, any thing without the *Bishop*.

Some indeed call him *Bishop*; yet do all things without him; but these seem not to me to have a good Conscience, but rather to be Hypocrites and Scorners.

I Exhort you to do all things in the same mind of God, the *Bishop* Presiding in the Place of *God*, and the *Presbyters* in room of the *College* of the *Apostles*, and the *Deacons*, most beloved to me, who are intrusted with the Ministry of *Jesus Christ*.

He directs his Epistle to the *Church* at *Philadelphia*, to those who were in Unity with their *Bishop* and *Presbyters* and *Deacons*.

And says to them, in his Epistle, *That* as many as are of *Christ*, these are with the *Bishop*; and those who shall Repent, and Return to the Unity of the *Church*, being made worthy of *Jesus Christ*, shall partake of Eternal Salvation in the Kingdom of *Christ*.

My Brethren, be not deceived, if any shall follow him that makes a *Schism*, he shall not Inherit the Kingdom of God.

I Exhort you to partake of the one *Eucharist*; for ther is one *Body* of the Lord *Jesus*, and one *Blood* of His, which was shed for us; and one *Cup*——and one *Altar*, so ther

ἔγνων καὶ τοὺς ἁγίους πρεσβυτέρους ————

Ὥσπερ ἓν ὁ Κύριος ἄνευ τοῦ Πατρὸς οὐδὲν ποιεῖ, ὅτῳ καὶ ὑμεῖς ἄνευ τοῦ Ἐπισκόπου, μηδὲ πρεσβύτερος, μηδὲ Διάκονος, μηδὲ λαικός.

Εἴ τινες Ἐπίσκοπον μὲν λέγουσι, χωρὶς ἢ αὐτῷ πάντα ποιοῦσιν —— Οἱ γὰρ τοιοῦτοι οὐκ εὐσυνείδητοι, ἀλλ᾿ εἴρωνές τινες καὶ μόρφωνες εἶ) μοι φαίνον).

παρακινῶ, ἐν ὁμονοίᾳ Θεοῦ σπουδάσατε πάντα πράττειν· προκαθημένου τοῦ Ἐπισκόπου εἰς τόπον Θεοῦ καὶ τῶν πρεσβυτέρων εἰς τόπον συνεδρίας τῶν Ἀποστόλων καὶ τῶν Διακόνων, τῶν ἐμοὶ γλυκυτάτων, πεπιστευμένων Διακονίαν Ἰησοῦ Χριστοῦ.

Ἐν ἑνὶ ὅσοι σὺν τῷ Ἐπισκόπῳ, καὶ τοῖς πρεσβυτέροις, καὶ Διακόνοις.

Ὅσοι γὰρ Χριστοῦ εἰσιν, οὗτοι μετὰ τοῦ Ἐπισκόπου εἰσίν· ὅσοι ἂν μετανοήσαντες ἔλθωσιν ἐπὶ τὴν Ἑνότητα τῆς Ἐκκλησίας, ἄξιοι Ἰησοῦ Χριστοῦ γινόμενοι, σωτηρίας αἰωνίου τεύξονται ἐν τῇ βασιλείᾳ τοῦ Χριστοῦ.

Ἀδελφοί, μὴ πλανᾶσθε· εἴ τις σχίζοντι ἀκολουθεῖ, βασιλείαν Θεοῦ οὐ κληρονομήσει.

παρακαλῶν ὑμᾶς μιᾷ Εὐχαριστίᾳ χρῆσθαι· μία γὰρ ἐστιν ἡ σὰρξ τοῦ Κυρίου Ἰησοῦ, καὶ ἓν αὐτοῦ τὸ αἷμα τὸ ὑπὲρ ἡμῶν ἐκχυθέν· εἷς καὶ Ἄρτος τοῖς πᾶσιν ἐθρύφθη——ἓν θυσιαστήρ-

is one *Bishop*, with his *Presbytery*, and the *Deacons*, my Fellow Servants.

Give heed to the *Bishop*, and to the *Presbytery*, and to the *Deacons*.—Without the *Bishop* do nothing.

In his Epistle to the Smyrneans, *he says*, Flee Divisions as the beginning of Evils. All of them follow their *Bishops*, as *Jesus Christ* the *Father*; and the *Presbyters*, as the *Apostles*, and Reverence the *Deacons* as the Institution of *God*. Let no man do any thing of what appertains to the *Church*, without the *Bishop*, Let that *Sacrament* be judg'd Effectual and Firm, which is Dispenced by the *Bishop*, or him to whom the *Bishop* has Committed it. Wherever the *Bishop* is, there let the *People* be; as where *Christ* is, there the *Heavenly Host* is gathered together. It is not lawful, without the *Bishop*, either to *Baptize*, or celebrate the *Offices*: But what He approves of, according to the good Pleasure of God, that is firm and safe, and so we do every thing securely.

I salute your most worthy *Bishop*, your venerable *Presbytery*, and the *Deacons* my Fellow Servants.

In his Epistle to St. Policarp, Bishop of Smyrna, *and* Martyr, *who, together with himself, was* Disciple to *St.* John *the* Apostle, *and* Evangelist. He gives these Directions.

If any can remain in Chastity, to the glory of the Body of the Lord, let him remain without Boasting, if he Boast, he Perishes; and if he pretends to know more than the

B ſhrp he is corrupted. It is the duty both of Men and Women that Marry, to be joyn'd together by the Approbation of the *Biſh.* that the Marriage may be in the Lord, and not according to our own Luſts. Glory of God.

Ζοῖς γαμῶσι, καὶ ζ̄ γαμύσαις, μ̄ γνώμης ζ̄ Ἐπισκόπε τῆν ἕνωσιν ποιεῖϑαι, ἵνα ὁ γάμⒼ ᾖ κ̄ Κύριον, καὶ μὴ κατ᾽ ἐπιϑυμίαν· πάντα εἰς τιμὴν Θεῦ γινέϑω.

Let all things be done to the Glory of God.

Give heed to your *Biſhop,* that God may Harken unto you: My Soul for theirs, who ſubject themſelves under the Obedience of their *Biſhop, Presbyters, and Deacons,* and let me take my Lot with them in the Lord.

Τῷ Ἐπισκόπῳ προσέχετε, ἵνα καὶ ὁ Θεὸς ὑμῖν. αντίψυχον ἐγὼ τῷ ὑποτασσομένων Ἐπισκόπῳ, πρεσβυτέρῳ, Διακόνοις· μετ᾽ αὐτῶν μοι τὸ μέρⒼ γένοιτο ἔχειν πρὸς Θεῦ.

And he ſays to Biſhop *Policarp. Let nothing be done without thy ſentence and approbation.*

Μηδὲν ἄνευ ζ̄ γνώμης σε γινέϑω.

A.D. 180. St. *Irenæus,* Biſhop of *Lyons,* in *France,* who was Diſciple of St. *Poiycarp;* he flouriſh'd about the year of *Chriſt* 180.

We can reckon thoſe *Biſhops,* who have been Conſtituted by the *Apoſtles,* and their Succeſſors all the way to our times. And if the Apoſtles knew hidden Myſteries, they wou'd certainly deliver them, chiefly to thoſe, to whom they committed the Churches themſelves; and whom they left their own Succeſſors, and in the ſame Place of Government as themſelves. We have the Succeſſions of the Biſhops, to whom the Apoſtolick Church in every place was committed. All theſe (*Heretcks*) are much later than the Biſhops, to whom the Apoſtles did deliver the Churches.

Advers. Hæreſes. l. 3. c. 3.

Habemus munerare qui ab Apoſtolis Inſtituti ſunt Epiſcopi in Eccleſiis, & ſucceſſores eorum uſque ad nos. Et ſi Recondita myſteria Sciiſſent. Apoſtoli, vel his maxime traderent ea, quibus etiam ipſas Eccleſias committebant; quos & ſucceſſores relinquebant, ſuum ipſorum locum Magiſterii tradentes. lib. 4. c. 63. Habemus ſucceſſiones Epiſcoporum quibus Apoſtolicam quæ in unoquoque loco eſt Eccleſiam tradiderunt. l. 5. c. 20. Omnes enim ii (Hæretici) valde Poſteriores ſunt, quam Epiſcopi, quibus Apoſtoli tradiderunt Eccleſias.

The true Knowledge is the Doctrin of the Apoſtles, and the Ancient State of the Church, through the whole World, and the Character of the Body

L. 4. c. 6. Agnitio vera eſt, Apoſtolorum Doctrina, & Antiquus Eccleſiæ ſtatus, in univerſo Mundo, & Character Corporis Chriſti ſecundum ſucceſſiones Epiſcoporum,

of

of Christ, according to the Succession of the Bishops, to whom they committed the Church that is in every Place; and which has Descended even unto us.

quibus illi eam quæ in unoquoq; loco est Ecclesiam tradiderunt, quæ pervenit usque ad nos.

Tertullian, A. D. 203. of the Prescription of *Hereticks.*

c. 32. Let them produce the Original of their Churches; let them shew the Order of their Bishops, that by their Succession, deduc'd from the beginning, we may see whether their first Bishop had any of the Apostles or Apostolical Men, who did likewise persevere with the Apostles, for his Founder and Predecessor. For, thus the Apostolical Churches do derive their Succession: As the Church of *Smyrna* from *Polycarp,* whom *John* (the Apostle) placed there: The Church of *Rome* from *Clement,* who was, in like manner, ordain'd by *Peter:* And so the other Churches can produce those Constituted in their *Bishopricks* by the *Apostles.*

Edant ergo Origines Ecclesiarum suarum; evolvant ordinem Episcoporum suorum, ita ut per successiones ab initio decurrentem, ut primus ille Episcopus aliquem ex Apostolis, vel Apostolicis viris, qui tamen cum Apostolis perseveraverit, habuerit Auctorem & Antecessorem. Hoc enim modo Ecclesiæ Apostolicæ census suos deferunt: sicut Smyrneorum *Ecclesia* Polycarpum *ab* Johanne *conlocatum refert; sicut* Romanorum, Clementem, *à* Petro *ordinatum itidem, perinde utique & Ceteræ exhibent quos ab Apostolis in Episcopatum Constitutos Apostolici seminis traduces habeant.*

c. 36. Reckon over the Apostolical Churches, where the very Chairs of the Apostles do yet Preside in their own Places. At *Corinth, Philippi, Ephesus, Thessalonica,* &c.

Percurre Ecclesias Apostolicas, apud quas ipsæ adhuc Cathedræ Apostolorum suis locis Præsident. Corinthi, Philippi, Ephesiis, Thessalonica, &c.

Of Baptism, *c.* 17.

The *High-Priest,* who is the *Bishop,* has the Power of conferring Baptism; and under him the *Presbyters* and *Deacons;* but not without the Authority of the *Bishop.*

Dandi (Baptismum) jus habet summus sacerdos, qui est Episcopus, *dehinc* Presbyteri *& Deacon, non tamen sine* Episcopi *Authoritate.*

Origen, Names the distinct Orders of *Bishop, Presby-*

A.D. 220. *Origenis Comment. in* Matt. *Rothomagi* 668. *Gr. Lat. p.* 255 *ter,*

A.D. 2

A.D. 220

ter, and *Deacon.* Such a Bishop (*says he, speaking of one who fought vain Glory,* &c.) doth not desire a good Work——and the same is to be said of *Presbyters* and *Deacons.——.*The *Bishops* and *Presbyters* who have the Chief Place among the People.——.The *Bishop* is called *Prince* in the *Churches*: And speaking of the Irreligious *Clergy,* he directs it to them, whether *Bishops,* *Presbyters,* or *Deacons.*

ὁ γὲν τοιοῦτος 'Επίσκοπ@. ὑ καλοῦ ἔργου ἐπιθυμεῖ — τὸ ϑ αὐτὸ καὶ πεϱὶ πρεσβυτέϱχν —— καὶ Διακόνων ἐϱῶ. *Ibid.* p. 443. οἱ ϑ τοῖς πϱοϱαβεθέι-ας πεπιςόμμένοι τῷ λαῷ 'Επίσκοπι καὶ Πϱεσβύτεϱοι. — p. 420 ὁ ϑ ἡγύ-μμ@., ὅτῳ ϑ οἴμαι ὀνομάζειν τ' καλόμμον ἐν τ¹ 'Εκλησίαις 'Επίσκο-πον.—— p. 442. 'Επισκόποις, ἢ πϱεσβυτέϱοις ἢ Διακόνοις.

D. 240.

St. *Cyprian* Archbishop of *Carthage,* A. D. 240.

Our Lord, whose Commands we ought to Reverence and Obey, being about to Constitute the *Episcopal* Honour, and the Frame of His Church, said to Peter, *Thou art Peter,*&c. From thence the Order of *Bishops* and Constitution of the Church does descend, by the line of Succession, thro' all Times and Ages; that the Church shou'd be built upon the *Bishops* — It is Establish'd by the Divine Law, that every Act of the Church shou'd be Govern'd by the Bishop. To Cornelius, *then Bishop of Rome.*

We ought chiefly (my Brother) to Endeavour to keep that Unity which was Enjoyn'd by our Lord and His Apostles to us their Successors, to be carefully observ'd by us.

The *Deacons* ought to remember that it was the *Lord* who chose the *Apostles,* that is, the *Bishops.*

Christ said to the *Apostles,* and by that, to all *Bishops* or Go-

Edit. Oxon. Epist. XXXIII. Lapsis.

Dominus noster, cujus Præcepta metuere & observare debemus, Episcopi honorem & Ecclesiæ suæ Rationem disponens, in Evangelio loquitur & dicit Petro, Ego dico tibi quia tu es Petrus, &c. *Inde per temporum & successionum vices Episcoprum Ordinatio & Ecclesiæ Ratio decurrit, ut Ecclesia super Episcopos Constituatur.——Divina Lege fundatum est, ut omnis actus Ecclesiæ per Episcopum Gubernetur.*

Ep. XLV. Cornelio.

Hoc enim vel maxime, Frater, & laborámus & laborare debemus, ut Unitatem à Domino, & per Apostolos nobis Successoribus traditam, quantum possumus obtinere curemus.

Ep. III. Rogatiano.

Meminisse autem Diaconi debent quoniam Apostolos, id est Episcopos Dominus Elegit.

Ep. LXVI. Florentio.

Dixit Christus ad Apostolos, ac vernors

vernors of His Church, who fucceed the *Apostles*, by vicarious
Ordination, and are in their
ſtead, *He that heareth you, heareth me.*

For from hence do Schiſms
and Hereſies ariſe, and have ariſen, while the *Biſhop*, who is
One, and *Governour* of the
Church, by a proud Preſumpti-
on is Deſpiſ'd; and that Man who
is Honour'd as Worthy by God,
is accounted unworthy by Man.

Nor are Hereſies ſprung up,
or Schiſms ariſen from any other
Fountain than from hence, that
Obedience is not paid to the
Prieſt of God ; and that ther is
not one *Prieſt* at a time in the
Church, and one Judge for the
time in the Place of Chriſt. To
whom if the whole Fraternity
did obey, according to the Divine Oeconomy, none wou'd
dare to move any thing againſt
the *Sacerdotal Colledge*----It is neceſſary that the *Biſhops* ſhou'd ex-
ert their Authority with full Vi-
gor---But if it is ſo, that we are
afraid of the Boldneſs of the
moſt Profligat ; and that which
theſe wicked Men cannot com-
paſs by the Methods of Truth
and Equity, if they can accom-
pliſh by their Raſhneſs and Deſ-
pair, then is ther an end of the
Epiſcopal Authority, and of their
Sublime and *Divine Power* in
Governing of the *Church*. Nor

*per hoc, ad omnes Prapoſitos, qui
Apoſtolis vicaria ordinatione ſucce-
dunt, Qui vos audit, me audit.——*

Ibid.

*Inde enim Schiſmata & Here-
ſes orta & oriuntur, dum Epiſco-
pus qui unus eſt, & Eccleſia Pra-eſt,
ſuperba Praſumptione contemni-
tur, & homo dignatione Dei ho-
noratus, Indignus hominibus judi-
catur.*

Ep. LIX. Cornelio.

*Neque enim aliunde Hereſes
oborta ſunt, aut nata ſunt ſchiſ-
mata, quam inde quod Sacerdoti
Dei non obtemperatur ; nec unus
in Eccleſia ad tempus Sacerdos,
& ad tempus Judex vice Chriſti cogitatur : Cui ſi ſecundum
Magiſteria Divina obtemperaret
Fraternitas univerſa, nemo ad-
verſus ſacerdotum Collegium
quicquam moveret——— vigore
pleno Epiſcopos agere oportet —
quod ſi ita res eſt ut Nequiſſimo-
rum timeatur Audacia, & quod
Mali vere atque æquitate non
poſſunt, Temeritate & Deſpera-
tione perficiant ; actum eſt de
Epiſcopatus vigore, & de Eccleſie gubernanda ſublimi ac Divina Poteſtate. Nec Chriſtiani
ultra aut durare aut eſſe jam poſ-
ſumus, ſi ad hoc ventum eſt, ut
Perditorum Minas atque Inſidias
pertimeſcamus —*

can

(44)

can we remain *Christians* any longer, if it is come to this, that we shou'd be afraid of the *Threats*, and *Snares* of the *wicked*---

---The Adversary of Christ, and Enemy of His Church, for this end strikes at the *Bishop* or *Ruler* of the *Church*, with all his Malice, that the *Governor* being taken away, he might Ravage the more Violently and Cruelly upon the Ship-wreck of the Church---

Is Honour then given to God, when the Divine Majesty and Censure is so Despised, that these Sacrilegious Persons say; do not think of the Wrath of God, be not afraid of His Judgment, do not knock at the Door of the Church; but without any Repentance, or Confession of their Crime, Despising the Authority of their *Bishops*, and trampling it under their feet, a False Peace is Preach'd to be had from the *Presbyters* (Scilicet) in their taking upon them to Admit those that were *Fallen* into *Communion*, or the *Peace* of the *Church*, without the Allowance of the *Bishop*.

---Christi Adversarius & Ecclesiæ ejus Inimicus, ad hoc Ecclesiæ Præpositum sua Infestatione persequitur, ut Gubernatore sublato, atrocius atque violentius circa Ecclesiæ Naufragia grassetur.---

Honor ergo datur Deo, quando sic Dei Majestas & Censura Contemnitur---ut proponatur à Sacrilegis atque dicatur; ne Ita cogitetur Dei, ne timeatur Judicium Domini, ne pulsetur ad Ecclesiam Christi, sed sublata Pœnitentia, nec ulla Exomologesi Criminis facta, Despectis Episcopis atque Calcatis, Pax à Presbyteris verbis fallacibus Prædicetur?

ibid.

They imitate the coming of Anti-Christ now approaching.

Antichristi jam propinquantis adventum imitantur.

Ep. LXXX. Successo.

Valerian (the Emperor) wrote to the Senate, that the *Bishops*, and the *Presbyters*, and the *Deacons* shou'd be prosecuted.

Rescripsisse valerianum ad Senatum, ut Episcopi, & Presbyteri, & Diacones in continenti animadvertantur.

Firmilianus Cypriano. Ep. LXXV. p. 225.

The Power of Remitting Sins, was given to the *Apostles*, and to the *Bishops*, who have succeeded them by a vicarious Ordination.

Potestas ergo Peccatorum remittendorum Apostolis data est - & Episcopis qui eis Ordinatione vicaria successerunt.

What

What Danger ought we to fear from the Displeasure of God, when some *Presbyters,* neither mindful of the Gospel, nor of their own Station in the Church, neither regarding the future Judgment of God, nor the *Bishop* who is set over them, which was never done under our Predecessors, with the Contempt and Neglect of their *Bishop,* do arrogate all unto themselves? I cou'd bear with the Contempt of our *Episcopal* Authority, but ther is now no room left for Dissembling, *&c.*

Optatus *Milevitanus,* Bishop of *Mileve,* or *Mela* in *Numidia* in *Africa.* A. D. 365.

In his 2d. Book against *Parmenian.* The Church has her several Members, *Bishops, Presbyters, Deacons,* and the Company of the Faithful.

You found in the Church, *Deacons, Presbyters, Bishops,* you have made them *Lay-men;* acknowledge that you have Subverted Souls.

St. *Ambrose* Bishop of *Milan.* A. D. 370. upon *Eph.* iv. 11. Speaking of *the several Orders of the Church. And he gave some* Apostles, and some Prophets, and Evangelists, &c. Says, that by the *Apostles* there were meant the *Bishops;* by *Prophets,* the Expounders of the *Scriptures;* and by the *Evangelists,* the *Deacons.* But says that they all met in the *Bishop;* for that he was the *Chief Priest,* that is,

Ep. XVI. p. 36. Cyprianus Presbyteris & Diaconibus.

Quod enim periculum metuere non debemus de offensa Domini; quando aliqui de Presbyteris, nec Evangelii, nec Loci sui memores, sed neque futurum Domini Judicium, neque sibi præpositum Episcopum *cogitantes, quod nunquam omnino sub Antecessoribus factum est, cum Contumelia & Contemptu Præpositi totum sibi vendicent?* Contumeliam Episcopatus *nostri dissimulare & ferre possum——sed dissimulandi nunc locus non est.*

1. 2. Contra Parmenianum. *Certa Membra sua habet. Ecclesia,* Episcopos, Presbyteros, Diaconos, *& turbam Fidelium.*

Invenistis Diaconos, Presbyteros, Episcopos *fecistis Laicos; agnoscite vos animas evertisse.*

Quosdam dedit Apostolos; quosdam Prophetas, *&c. Apostoli,* Episcopi *sunt: Prophetæ Explanatores sunt Scripturam sicut* Agabus——*Evangelistæ* Diaconi *sunt, sicut fuit* Philippus.——*Nam in* Episcopo *omnes ordines sunt, quia* Princeps Sacerdos *est, hoc est,* Princeps est Sacerdotum, *&* Propheta, *&* Evangelista, *& Cætera adimplenda officia Ecclesiæ in Ministerio Fidelium.*

(says

(*says he*) the *Prince* of the *Priefts*, and both *Prophet* and *Evangelift*, to fupply all the Offices of the Church for the Miniftry of the Faithful.

And upon 1 *Cor.* xii. 28. fays that *Chrift* Conftituted the *Apoftles Head* in the *Church*; and that thefe are the *Bifhops*.

Caput in Ecclefia Apoftolos pofuit ——— *Ipfi funt* Epifcopi.

And upon *v.* 29. are all *Apoftles?* i. e. all are not *Apoftles.* This is true (*fays he,*) becaufe in the Church ther is but one *Bifhop.*

Verum eft, quia in Ecclefia unus Epifcopus *eft.*

And becaufe all things are from one God the Father, therefore hath He appointed that one *Bifhop* fhou'd Prefide over Each Church.

Quia ab uno Deo Patre funt omnia, fingulos Epifcopos, fingulis Ecclefiis Præ-effe Decrevit.

In his Book of the *Dignity* of the *Priefthood*, c. 3. he fays, That ther is nothing in this World to be found more *Excellent* than the *Priefts*, nothing more *Sublime* than the *Bifhops.*

De Dignat. Sacerdot. c. 3. ut oftenderemus nihil effe in hoc feculo Excellentius Sacerdotibus, *nihil Sublimius* Epifcopis *reperiri.*

And fpeaking of what was Incumbent upon the feveral Orders of the *Church*, he does plainly diftinguifh them : For, fays he, in the fame place ;

God does require one thing from a *Bifhop*, another from a *Presbyter*, another from a *Deacon*, and another from a *Lay-man.*

Aliud eft enim quod ab Epifcopo *requirit Deus, & aliud quod à* Presbytero, *& aliud quod à* Deacono, *& aliud quod à* Laico.

80. St. *Jerom*, A. D. 380. In his Comment upon the Ep. to *Titus.*

When it began to be faid, *I am of Paul, I of Apollos,* &c. and every one thought that thofe whom he Baptized, belong'd to himfelf, and not to Chrift; it was Decreed thro' *The whole Earth*, that one Chofen from among the *Presbyters* fhou'd be fet over the reft, that the Seeds of *Schifm* might be taken away.

Poftquam unufquifque eos quos Baptizabat fuos putabat effe non Chrifti, IN TOTO ORBE *Decretum eft, ut unus de* Presbyteris *Electus fuperponeretur Cæteris, ut Schifmatum femina tollerentur.*

In his *Epift.* to *Evagrius.*

From *Mark* the *Evangelift* to *Heraclas,* and *Dionyfius* the *Bifhops*, the Presbyters of Egypt have

A Marco *Evangelifta ad* Heraclum ufq; ad Dionyfium *Epifcopos, Presbyteri* Ægypti *femper unum ex fe Electum, in Clefiori Gra-*

always chofen out one from a-mong themfelves, whom hav-ing plac'd in an higher Degree than the reft, they called their *Bifhop*.

du collocatum Epifcopum *Nomina-bant.*

He that is Advanc'd, is Ad-vanc'd from lefs to greater.

Qui provehitur, à Minori ad Ma-jus provehitur.

The Greatnefs of Riches, or the Humility of Poverty does not make a *Bifhop* greater or lefs, fee-ing *all* of them are the *Succeffors* of the *Apoftles.*

Fotentia Divitiarum & Pauper-tatis Humilitas, fublimiorem vel inferiorem Epifcopum *non facit, Ceterum Omnes* Apoftolorum *Suc-ceffores funt.*

That we may know the Apo-ftolical Oeconomy to be taken from the Pattern of the Old Te-ftament, the fame that *Aaron,* and his *Sons,* and the *Levites* were in the *Temple,* the *Bifhops,* *Presbyters,* and *Deacons* are in the *Church* of *Chrift:*

Ut fciamus Traditiones Apoftoli-cas fumptas de veteri Teftamento: Quod Aaron, *& Filii ejus atq;* Levitæ *in* Templo *fuerunt, hoc fibi* Epifcopi, Presbyteri, *&* Deaconi., *vendicent in* Eccle-fia.

To *Nepotianus.*

Ad Nepotianum.

Be fubject to your *Bifhop* or *Chief-Prieft* ; and receive him as the Father of your Soul.

Efto fujectus Pontifici *tuo* ; *& quafi animi* Parentem *fufcipe.*

Againft the *Luciferians.*

Adverf. Luciferianos.

The fafety of the Ch. depends upon the Dignity of the *High-Prieft,* to whom unlefs a fort of abfolute and eminent Power be given above all, ther will be as many *Schifms* in the *Church* as ther are *Priefts.* Thence it is, that without the Command of the *Bifhop,* neither a *Presbyter,* nor a *Deacon,* have Power to Bap-tize---- And the *Bifhop* is to im-pofe his Hands upon thofe who are Baptized by *Presbyters* or *Dea-cons,* for the Invocation of the Holy Spirit.

Ecelafiæ falus in fummi Sa-cerdotis *Dignitate pendet, cui ni-fi exors quædam & ab omnibus Eminens detur Poteftas, tot in Ec-clæfia efficientur Schifmata quot Sacerdotes. Inde venit, ut fine E-*pifcopi *juffione neque* Presbyter *neque* Diaconus *jus habeant Bap-tizandi----Ad eos qui per* Presby-teros *&* Diaconos *Baptizati funt,* Epifcopus *ad Invocationem fancti Spiritus manum Impofiturus ex-currat.*

And Comforting *Heliodorus,* a *Bifhop,* upon the Death of *Nepo-*

Epitaphium Nepotiani à Helio-dorum. *Epifcopum venerebatur----* *tian-*

than his Presbyter and his Ne-
phew, he Commends *Nepotian* in
that he Reverenc'd his *Bishop.* He
Honour'd *Heliodorus,* in publick
as his *Bishop,* at home as his Father.
and *Co-equals,* he was the first in his Vocation, &c.

In publico Episcopum, *domi* Pa-
trem noverat.---Inter Presbyteros
& Co-*æquales, primus in opere,*
&c.

But among his *Presbyters*

Upon the *60th.* of *Isa.* He calls
the future *Bishops, Princes* or the
Church.

Principes futuros. Ecclefiæ Epifcopos *Nominav.t.*

Of the Ecclesiastical Writers.
Concerning *James.*

In script. Ecclesiast. De Ja-
cobo.

James, after the Passion of our
Lord, was immediatly, by, the
Apostles, ordained Bishop of *Je-
rusalem.* The like he tells of the

*Jacobus post. Passionem Domini
statim ab Apostolis Hierosolimorum
Episcopus est ordinatus.*
first Bishops of other Places.

Epist. 54. against *Montanus.*
With us the *Bishops* hold the
Place of the *Apostles.*

Ep. 54, *contra* Montanum.
Apud nos Apostolorum *locum*
Episcopi*tenent.*

St. Augustine *Bishop* of *Hippo* in *Africa,* A. D. 420. Epistle 42.

The Root of the Christian Society is diffus'd throughout the
World, in a sure Propagation,
by the Seats of the *Apostles,* and
the Succession of the *Bishops.*
Quest. veter. & novi Test. N. 97.

*Radix Christianæ Societatis per
sedes* Apostolorum & *Successiones*
Episcoporum *certa per orbem Pro-
pagatione diffunditur.*

Ther is none but knows that
our Saviour did Constitute Bishops in the Churches; for before He Ascended into Heaven,
He laid His Hands upon the A-
postles and Ordained them Bishops.

Nemo ignorat Salvatorem Epifcopos *Ecclesiis Instituisse; Ipse enim
priusquam Cælos Ascenderet, Impo-
nens Manus* Apostolis *ordinavit
eos* Episcopos, *Quod dixit* Clarus
à Muscula *in Concilio* Carthag. *Re-
petit* August. *de Baptismo contra*
Donatist.

l. 7. c. 43. The Sentence of
our Lord Jesus Christ is clear,
who sent His Apostles, and gave
to *Them alone* that Power which
He had Received from His Fa-

*Manifesta est sententia Domi-
ni nostri* Jesu Christi *Apostolos
suos, mittentis, & ipsis solis
Potestatem à Patre sibi traditam permittentis; quibus, nos-*
ther;

Father, to whom we have Succeeded, Governing the Church of God by the same Power.

nos Succeſſimus, eadem Poteſtate Eccleſiam Domini Gubernantes.

Ep. 162. *speaking of the* Bishops *being call'd Angels. Rev.* 2. *he says,*

By the voice of God, the Governor of the Church is Praised, under the Name of an *Angel.*

Divina voce sub nomine Angeli Laudatur Præpositus Eccleſie.

Of the words of our Lord, Serm. 24.

If He said to the Apostles alone, *he that despiseth you, despiseth me,* then despise us: But if those words of His come down even unto us, and that He has Called us, and Constituted us in their Place, see that you do not despise us.

De verbis Domini, Serm. 24.

Si solis Apostolis dixit, Qui vos spernit, me spernit, *spernite nos: Si autem Sermo Ejus pervenit ad nos, & vocavit nos, & in eorum loco Constituit nos, videte ne spernatis nos.*

Against *Fauſtus.*

We embrace the Holy Scripture, which from the Times of the Presence of Christ himself, by the Disposition of the Apostles, and the Successions of other *Biſhops* from their Seats, even to these Times, has come down to us, safely kept, commended and honour'd through the whole Earth.

Contra Fauſt. *Lib.* 33. *cap.* ult.

Scripturam amplectimur quæ ab Ipſius Preſentia Chriſti temporibus, per Diſpenſationes Apoſtolorum, & cæteras ab eorum ſedibus Succeſſiones Episcoporum, uſque ad hæc tempora toto Orbe terrarum cuſtodita, commendata, clarificata pervenit.

Against Petilian.

What has the Chair of the Church of *Rome* done to thee, in which *Peter* sat, and in which, at this day, *Anaſtaſius* sits; or of the Church of *Jeruſalem*, in which *James* did sit, and in which *John* does now sit.

Lib. 2. *contra Literas Petiliani* C. 51.

Cathedra quid tibi fecit Eccleſiæ Romanæ *in qua* Petrus *ſedit; & in qua hodie* Anaſtaſius *ſedet; aut Eccleſiæ* Hieroſolimitanæ *in qua* Jacobus *ſedit, & in qua hodie* Joannes *ſedet.* [*Vid. contra* Creſcon. *l.* 2. *c.* 37.]

Against Julian.

Irenæus, Cyprian, Reticius, Olympius, Hilary, Gregory, Ba-

Contra Julianum, *l.* 2, *cap.* últ.

Irenæus, Cyprianus, Reticius, Olympius, Hilarius, Gregorius,

H   ſil,

fil, John, Ambrofe— thefe were *Bifhops*, Grave, Learned, &c.

Bafilius, Joannes, Ambrofius, ifti erant Epifcopi, Docti; Graves, &c. in Ecclefia Regimine Clari.

Queftions upon the Old Teftament. Queft. 35.

Queft. ex vet. Teft. qu. 35.

The *King* bears the Image of *God*, as the *Bifhop* of *Chrift*. Therefore while he is in that Station, he is to be Honour'd, if not for himfelf, yet for his Order.

Dei enim Imaginem habet Rex, *ficut &* Epifcopus Chrifti. *Quamdiu ergo in ea traditione eft, Honorandus eft, fi non propter fe, vel propter Ordinem.*

Let this fuffice as to the Teftimonies of particular *Fathers* of the Church, tho' many more may be produc'd, in that compafs of time, to which I have confin'd our prefent Inquiry. And now (that no Conviction might be wanting) I will fet down fome of the *Canons* of the *Councils* in thofe times, to the fame purpofe; whereby it will appear, that *Epifcopacy*, as *diftinct* from, and *fuperior* to *Presbytery*, was not only the Judgment of the firft Glorious *Saints* and *Martyrs* of *Chrift*; but the current *Doctrin*, and *Government* of the *Church*, both *Greek* and *Latin*, in thofe early Ages of *Chriftianity*.

In the *Canons* of the *Apoftles*, the diftinction of *Bifhop*, *Presbyter*, and *Deacon* is fo frequent, that it is almoft in vain to give *Citations*. The 1ft. and 2d. *Can.* fhew the difference to be obferv'd in the *Ordaining* of them.

Let a *Bifhop* be Confecrated by two or three *Bifhops*.

Ἐπίσκοπ Θ χειροτονείσθω ὑπὸ Ἐπισκόπων δύο ἢ τριῶν.

Let a *Presbyter* and *Deacon* be Ordained by one *Bifhop*.

πρεσβύτερ Θ ὑπὸ ἑνὸς Ἐπισκόπου χειροτονείσθω, ὁ Διάκον Θ.

See the fame Diftinction of thefe Orders. *Can.* 3. 4, 5, 6, 7, 8. 17, 18. 25. 27, 28, 29. 32, 33. 36. 42. 44, 45. 51, 52, 53. 63. 68, 69, 70. 83. *Can.* 15. fhews the Jurifdiction of the *Bifhops* over the *Presbyters* and *Deacons*.

If any *Presbyter* or *Deacon*, or any of the *Clerical* Order, fhall leave his own Parifh, and go to another, without the *Bifhop's* leave, he fhall officiate no longer; efpecially if he obey not the *Bifhop*, when he exhorts him to Return, perfifting in his Infolence

Εἴ τις πρεσβύτερ Θ, ἢ Διάκον Θ, ἢ ὅλως τῷ καταλόγῳ τῶ Κληρικῶν, ἀπολείψας τ ἑαυτῷ παροικίαν, εἰς ἑτέραν ἀπέλθη, καὶ πάντελῶς μεταςὰς δια τε ῖ ἐν ἄλλη παροικία παρὰ γνώμω τ ιδίε Ἐπισκόπε· τῦτον κελεύομεν μηκέτι λειτεργῖν, εἰ μάλιςα προσκαλεμένε αὐτὸν τῦ Ἐπισκόπε αὐτῷ,

and

and diſorderly Behaviour, but he ſhall be reduc'd there to Communicate only as a Lay-man.

And *Can.* 31. If any *Presbyter*, deſpiſing his own *Biſhop*, ſhall gather Congregations apart, and erect another Altar, his *Biſhop* not being Convict of Wickedneſs or Irreligion, let him be Depos'd as an Ambitious Perſon; for, he is a Tyrant: And likewiſe ſuch other *Clergy* or *Laity*, who ſhall joyn themſelves to him ſhall be Excommunicated. But, let this be after the firſt, ſecond, and third Admonition of the *Biſhop*.

Can. 39. Let the *Presbyters* and *Deacons* do nothing without the Conſent of the *Biſhop*; for it is He to whom the People of the Lord are committed, and from whom an account of their Souls will be Requir'd.

Can. 41. We Ordain the *Biſhop* to have power of the Goods of the Church— And to Adminiſter to thoſe who want, by the hands of the *Presbyters* and *Deacons*.

Can. 55. If any *Clergy man* ſhall Reproach his *Biſhop*, let him be Depos'd: For, *Thou ſhalt not ſpeak Evil of the Ruler of the People.*

After the *Canons* of the *Apoſtles*, I produce next a Great Council of 87 Biſhops held at *Carthage*, in the Year of *Chriſt*, 256, under St. *Cyprian*, Archbiſhop of that Place, which is Publiſhed in St. *Cyprian's* Works before quoted, p. 229. where he tells us,

That beſides the *Biſhops*, ther met there both *Presbyters* and *Epiſcopi plurimi cum Presbyteris & Diaconibus*, &c.

The Council of *Eliberis* in *Spain*, about the Year of *Christ* 305. Cap. 18. and 19.

Bishops, *Presbyters*, and *Deacons* are Nam'd distinct. And c. 32. *Presbyters* and *Deacons* are forbid to give the Communion to those who had grievously offended, without the Command of the Bishop.

Episcopi, *Presbyteri*, & *Diaconi*, &c. *Non est Presbyterorum, aut Diaconorum Communionem talibus præstare debere, nisi eis jusserit Episcopus.*

c. 75. Of those who shall falsly accuse a *Bishop*, *Presbyter*, or *Deacon*.

Si quis Episcopum, Presbyterum, vel Diaconum falsis Criminibus appetierit, &c.

c. 77. It is ordained that those who are Baptiz'd by a *Deacon*, without the *Bishop* or *Presbyter*, shall afterwards be Confirm'd by the *Bishop*.

Si quis Diaconus, sine Episcopo vel Presbytero aliquos Baptizaverit; Episcopus eos per Benedictionem perficere debebit.

The Council of *Arles* in *France*, about the Year of *Christ* 309. c. 18. It is ordain'd that the *Deacons* shou'd be subject to the *Presbyters*: And c. 19.

That the *Presbyters* shou'd be subject to their *Bishop*, and do nothing without his consent.

Presbyteri sine Conscientia Episcopi nihil faciant.

The Council of *Ancyra*, A. D. 315.

c. 1, and 2. Having Prohibited those *Presbyters* and *Deacons* who had, in times of Persecution, Offer'd to Idols, from the Execution of their Office, *says*, that notwithstanding the *Bishop* may Dispence with them if he sees their Repentance sincere; for that this Power is lodg'd in the *Bishop*.

Ἐι μέντοι τινὲς τῶν Ἐπισκόπων τούτοις συνίδοιεν κάματόν τινα ἢ ταπείνωσιν πραότητ(Θ), κ, ἐθέλοιεν πλέον τι διδόναι ἢ ἀφαιρεῖν, ἐπ᾽ αὐτοῖς εἴη τὴν ἐξουσίαν.

The Council of *Laodicea*, A. D. 321.

Can. 41. That no *Clergy-man* ought to Travel, without the consent of his *Bishop*.

Ὅτι ὁ δεῖ Ἱερατικὸν ἢ Κληρικὸν ἄνευ κελεύσεως Ἐπισκόπου ὁδεύειν.

Can. 56. That the *Presbyters* ought not to go into the Church, and sit in their Stales, till the *Bishop* come, and to go in with the *Bishop*.

Ὅτι ὀ δεῖ πρεσβυτέρους πρὸ τῆς εἰσόδου τῆ Ἐπισκόπου εἰσιέναι & καθέζεσθαι ἐν τῇ βήματι, ἀλλὰ μετὰ τῆ Ἐπισκόπου εἰσιέναι.

The First and Great Council of *Nice*, A. D. 325.

Can. 16. That if any *Presbyters* or *Deacons* leave their own Churches, they ought not to be receiv'd into another Church: And that if any shall ordain such in his Ch. as belong to another, without the consent of his proper *Bishop*, let such Ordination be void.

Πρεσβύτεροι ἢ Διάκονοι οἱ ἀναχωρήσαντι τ᾽ ἐκκλησίας, ἐδαμῶς δεκζοὶ ὀφείλασιν ἐἶ ἐν ἑτέρα ἐκκλησία —— εἰ ἢ κ᾽ ζολμήσειέν τις ὑπαρπάσαι τ᾽ τ᾽ ἑτέρῳ διαφέροντα, καὶ χειρο ζωἦσαι ἐν τῇ αὐτῇ ἐκκλησίᾳ, μὴ συγκαταἀθεμθέντος τῷ ἰδίῳ Ἐπισκόπῳ —— ἄκυρ Θ᾽ ἔσω ἡ χειροζωνία.

The Council of *Gangra*, 326.

Can. 6. If any have private Meetings out of the Church, without their *Presbyter*, let 'em be Anathematiz'd by the Sentence of the *Bishop*.

Ἔ᾽ τις πρὸ τῆ ἐκκλησίαν κατ᾽ ἰδίαν ἐκκλησιάζει —— μὴ σωόν Θ᾽ τῷ Πρεσβυτέρῳ, κᾳ᾽ γνώμῃ τῇ Ἐπισκόπῳ, ἀνάθεμα ἔσω.

Can. 7. If any will take or give of the Fruits offer'd to the Church, out of the Church, without leave of the *Bishop*, let him be *Anathema*.

Εἴ τις καρποφορίας ἐκκλησιαστικὰς ἐθέλῃ λαμβάνειν, ἢ διδόναι ἔξω τ᾽ ἐκκλησίας, πρὸ γνώμῃ τῷ Ἐπισκόπῳ —— Ἀνάθεμα ἔσω.

The Council of *Antioch*, A. D. 341.

Can. 3. If any *Presbyter* or *Deacon*, leaving his own Parish, shall go to others; and refuse to return, when his own *Bishop* shall summon him, let him be Depos'd.

Εἰ τις Πρεσβύτερ Θ᾽ ἢ Διάκον Θ᾽ καταλειπὼν τ᾽ ἑαυτῷ Παροικίαν, εἰς ἑτέραν ἀπέλθῃ, εἰ μάλιςα καλῶντι τῷ Ἐπισκόπῳ τῷ ἰδίῳ ἐπανελθεῖν εἰς τ᾽ παροικίαν τ᾽ ἑαυτῷ κ᾽ πρὸ φανέντι μὴ ὑπακάει —— παντελῶς αὐτὸν καθαιρεῖσθαι τ᾽ λειτεργίας.

Can. 4. If any *Bishop* being Depos'd by a *Synod*, or a *Presbyter* or *Deacon* being Depos'd by his own proper *Bishop*, shall presume to exercise his Function, let no room be left them, either

Εἴ τις Ἐπίσκοπ Θ᾽ ὑπὸ Συνόδε καθαιρεθεὶς, ἢ Πρεσβύτερ Θ᾽ ἢ Διάκον Θ᾽ ὑπὸ τ᾽ ἰδίε Ἐπισκόπε, ζολμήσειέν τι πεῖξαι τῆς λειτεργίας, μηδ᾽ ἀποκαταςάσεως, μηδ᾽ ἀπολογίας χώραν ἔχειν.

Can. 59. That one *Bishop* may ordain many *Presbyters*; but that it was hard to find a *Presbyter* who was fit to be made a *Bishop*.

Δύνα] ὁ εἷς Ἐπίσκοπος πολλὲς χειροτονεῖν Πρεσβύτερους· Πρεσβύτε-ρ@ ἢ πρὸς Ἐπισκοπὴν ὀπιτήδει@ δυσχερῶς εὑρίσκετ].

Can. 65. That a *Clergy man*, being Condemned by the *Bishops*, cannot be deliver'd by that *Church* to which he did belong, or by any Man whatsoever.

Κληρικὸν τῇ τ' Ἐπισκόπων κρίσι καταδικασθέντα, μὴ ἐξεῖναι τ' αὐτὸν εἴτε παρὰ τ' ἐκκλησίας, ἡς ὑπῆρ-χεν, εἴτε ἀπὸ οἱϣδήποτε Ἀνθρώπε δι-εκδικεῖϑαι ποινῆς.

Can. 126. That *Presbyters* and *Deacons* may Appeal from their own *Bishop* to the Neighbouring *Bishops*, chosen by consent of their own *Bishop*, and from them to the *Primate* or *Provincial Synod*; but not to any *Trans-marine* or *Forraign* Jurisdiction, under pain of Excommunication.

Πρεσβύτεροι, ἢ Διάκονοι, ἐν αἷς ἔχωσιν αἰτίας, ἐαν περὶ τ' ψήρα τὸς ἰδίας Ἐπισκόπες μέμφωντα, οἱ γείτνιῶντες Ἐπίσκοποι τέτων ἀκροά-σων], ἡ τὰ μεταξὺ τέτων πρατώ-σωσιν οἱ παρ' αὐτῷ ἢ ἐξμνάρεσιν τ ἰδίων αὐτῷ Ἐπισκόπων προσλαμ-βανόμροι· ἐαν ἢ ἡ ἀπ' αὐτῷ ἐκκα-λέσϑαι ϑελήσωσιν, μὴ ἐκκαλέσων], εἰ μὴ πρὸς τὰς τ' Ἀφρικῆς Συνόδες, ἢ πρὸς τὸς Πρωτεύοντας τῆ ἰδίων αὐτῷ ἐπαρχῶν. πρὸς ἢ τὰ πέραν τ' ϑαλάσσης ὁ Βελόμ@ ἐκκαλῶ@, ἀπὸ μηδενὸς ἐν Ἀφρικῆ δεχϑείη εἰς κοινωνίαν.

The Council of *Chalcedon*, being the Fourth General Council A. D. 451.

Can. 9. If any *Clergy-man* have a Cause of complaint against another *Clergy-man*, let him not leave his own proper *Bishop*, and have Recourse to the *Secular* Courts--Whoever does otherwise shall be put under the Canonical Censures.

Εἴ τις κληρικὸς πρὸς κληρικὸν πρᾶγμα ἔχοι, μὴ ἐγκαταλιμπαν-έτω τ' οἰκεῖον Ἐπίσκοπον, ἢ ὀπὶ κοσμικὰ δικαςήρια μὴ καταςρεχέ-τω―― εἰ ἢ τις παρὰ ταῦτα ποι-ήσοι, Κανονικοῖς ἐπιτιμίοις ὑποκεί-σϑω.

Can. 13. That a Forreign *Clergy-man*, and not known, shall not officiate in another City, without Commendatory Letters from his own *Bishop*.

Ξένες κληρικὸς ἢ ἀγνώςες ἐν ἑτέρα πόλει, δίχα συςατικῶν γραμ-μάτων τῷ ἰδίε Ἐπισκόπε μηδ' ὅλως μηϑαμῆ λειτεργεῖν.

Can. 18. If any of the *Clergy* shall be found Confpiring, or Joyning in *Fraternities*, or Contriving any thing againft the *Bishops*, they shall fall from their own Degree.

Εἴ τινες τοίνυν Κληρικοὶ ἢ Μοιάζοντες εὑρεθεῖεν ἢ ζωομνύμβοι ἢ Φρατριάζοντες, ἢ κατασκευὰς τυρεύοντες Επισκόποις, ἢ συγκλερικοῖς, ἐκπιπτέτωβ πάν]η τᾶ οἰκείε βαθμᾶ.

Can. 29. To reduce a *Bishop* to the Degree of a *Presbyter*, is Sacrilege.

Επίσκοπον εἰς Πρεσβυτέρε βαθμὸν Φέρειν Ἱεροσυλία ὄξίν.

Thefe Authorities are fo plain and full as to prevent any Application, or Multiplying of further Quotations, which might eafily be done: For, if thefe can be anfwer'd, fo may all that can poffibly be produc'd, or framed in words.

And ther is no Remedy left to the *Presbyterians*, and other Diffenters from *Epifcopacy*, but to deny all thefe by whole-fale, to throw off all *Antiquity*, as well the firft Ages of Chriftianity, even that wherein the *Apoftles* themfelves Liv'd and Taught, as all fince ; and to ftand upon a New Foundation of their own Invention.

But this only fhews the Defperatnefs of their Caufe ; and the Impregnable Bulwork of *Epifcopacy* ; which (I muft fay it) 'ftands upon fo *Many, Clear,* and *Authentick Evidences,* as can never be overthrown, but by fuch *Topicks* as muft render *Chriftianity* it felf Precarious.

And if from the *Etymology* of the Words *Bifhop* and *Presbyter,* any Argument can be drawn (againft all the Authorities Produc'd) to prove them the fame, we may, by this way of Reafoning, prove *Cyrus* to be *Chrift*, for fo he is call'd, *Ifa.* XLV. 1.

Or if the *Presbyterians* will have their *Moderator* to be a *Bifhop*, we will not Quarrel with them about a word. Let us then have a *Moderator*, fuch as the *Bifhops* before defcrib'd, *viz.* A *Moderator*, as a ftanding Officer, during *Life*, to whom all the *Presbyters* are to be obedient as to *Chrift*, *i. e.* to the *Moderator*, as Reprefenting the Perfon of *Chrift* : That nothing be done in the *Church* without Him : That He be underftood as the *Principle* of *Unity* in His *Church* ; fo that, they who unjuftly break off from his *Communion*, are thereby in a *Schifm* : That he fhew his *Succeffion*, by Regular Ordination, convey'd down from the *Apoftles*. In fhort, that He have all that *Character* and

I

Autho-

Can. 59. That one *Bishop* may ordain many *Presbyters*; but that it was hard to find a *Presbyter* who was fit to be made a *Bishop*.

Can. 65. That a *Clergy man*, being Condemned by the *Bishops*, cannot be deliver'd by that *Church* to which he did belong, or by any Man whatsoever.

Can. 126. That *Presbyters* and *Deacons* may Appeal from their own *Bishop* to the Neighbouring *Bishops*, chosen by consent of their own *Bishop*, and from them to the *Primate* or *Provincial Synod*; but not to any *Trans-marine* or *Forraign* Jurisdiction, under pain of Excommunication.

Δύνα)] ὁ εἷς Ἐπίσκοπς πολλὰς χειροτονεῖν Πρεσβύτερους· Πρεσβύτε ρ@, ἢ πρὸς Ἐπισκοπὴν ὀπιτήδει@ δυσχερῶς εὑρίσκετ).

Κλήεικὸν τῇ τ᾿ Ἐπισκόπων κρίσι καταδικαθέντα, μὴ ἐξεῖναι τ᾿ αὐτὸν εἴτε παρὰ τ᾿ ἐκκλησίας, ις ὑπῆρχεν, εἴτε ἀπὸ οἰσδήποτε Ἀνθρώπς δι εκδικεῖσθαι ποιεῖς.

Πρεσβύτεροι, ὁ Διάκονοι, ἐν αἷς ἔχωσιν αἰτίας, ἐαν περὶ τ᾿ ψήρα τὰς ἰδίας Ἐπισκόπας μέμφωνται, οἱ γείτονες Ἐπίσκοποι τούτων ἀκροάσων), ἡ τὰ μεταξὺ τούτων πεατώσωσιν οἱ παρ᾿ αὐτῷ κ᾿ ζυναίνεσιν τ᾿ ἰδίων αὐτῷ Ἐπισκόπων προσλαμβανόμοι· ἐαν ἢ ἡ ἀπ᾿ αὐτῷ ἐκκαλέσθαι θελήσωσιν, μὴ ἐκκαλείσθων),

εἰ μὴ πρὸς τὴς τ᾿ Ἀρχικῆς ζυνόδας, ἢ πρὸς τὰς Πρωτεύοντας τῆς ἰδίων αὐτῷ ἐπαρχιῶν. πρὸς ἢ τὰ πέραν τ᾿ θαλάσσης ὁ Βαλόμι@ ἐκκαλέσθ, ἀπὸ μηδενὸς ἐν Ἀφρικῇ δεχθεὶη εἰς κοινωνίαν.

The Council of *Chalcedon*, being the Fourth General Council A. D. 451.

Can. 9. If any *Clergy-man* have a Cause of complaint against another *Clergy-man*, let him not leave his own proper *Bishop*, and have Recourse to the *Secular* Courts--Whoever does otherwise shall be put under the Canonical Censures.

Can. 13. That a Forreign *Clergy-man*, and not known, shall not officiate in another City, without Commendatory Letters from his own *Bishop*.

Εἴ τις κληεικὸς πρὸς κληεικὸν πρᾶγμα ἔχοι, μὴ ἐγκαταλιμπανέτω τ᾿ οἰκεῖον Ἐπίσκοπον, ὁ ὀπὶ κοσμικὰ δικαστήεια μὴ κατατρεχέτω—— εἰ ἢ τις παρὰ ταῦτα ποιήσοι, Κανονικοῖς ἐπιτιμίοις ὑποκείσθω.

Ξένας κληεικὸς ὁ ἀγνώςας ἐν ἑτέρα πόλῳ, δίχα συστατικῶν γεαμμάτων τῷ ἰδίῳ Ἐπισκόπῳ μηδ᾿ ὅλως μηδαμᾷ λειτυργεῖν.

Can.

Can. 18. If any of the *Clergy* shall be found Confpiring, or Joyning in *Fraternities*, or Contriving any thing againſt the *Biſhops*, they ſhall fall from their own Degree.

Εἴ τινες τοίνυν Κληρικοὶ ἢ Μοιάζοντες εὑρεθεῖεν ἢ Ϲυωμνύμφοι ἢ Φρατριάζοντες, ἢ κατασκευὰς τυρεύοντες Ἐπισκόποις, ἢ συγκλητικῆς, ἐκπιπτέτωσ᾽ πάν᾿η τῷ οἰκείυ βαθμῷ.

Can. 29. To reduce a *Biſhop* to the Degree of a *Presbyter*, is *Sacrilege*.

Ἐπίσκοπον εἰς Πρεσβυτέρυ βαθμὸν φέρειν Ἱεροσυλία ἐϛὶν.

Theſe Authorities are ſo plain and full as to prevent any Application, or Multiplying of further Quotations, which might eaſily be done: For, if theſe can be anſwer'd, ſo may all that can poſſibly be produc'd, or framed in words.

And ther is no Remedy left to the *Presbyterians*, and other Diſſenters from *Epiſcopacy*, but to deny all theſe by whole-ſale, to throw off all *Antiquity*, as well the firſt Ages of Chriſtianity, even that wherein the *Apoſtles* themſelves Liv'd and Taught, as all ſince ; and to ſtand upon a New Foundation of their own Invention.

But this only ſhews the Deſperatneſs of their Cauſe ; and the Impregnable Bulwork of *Epiſcopacy* ; which (I muſt ſay it) ſtands upon ſo *Many*, *Clear*, and *Authentick Evidences*, as can never be overthrown, but by ſuch *Topicks* as muſt render *Chriſtianity* it ſelf Precarious.

And if from the *Etymology* of the Words *Biſhop* and *Presbyter*, any Argument can be drawn (againſt all the Authorities Produc'd) to prove them the ſame, we may, by this way of Reaſoning, prove *Cyrus* to be *Chriſt*, for ſo he is call'd, *Iſa.* XLV. 1.

Or if the *Presbyterians* will have their *Moderator* to be a *Biſhop*, we will not Quarrel with them about a word. Let us then have a *Moderator*, ſuch as the *Biſhops* before deſcrib'd, *viz.* A *Moderator*, as a ſtanding Officer, during *Life*, to whom all the *Presbyters* are to be obedient as to *Chriſt*, *i.e.* to the *Moderator*, as Repreſenting the Perſon of *Chriſt* : That nothing be done in the *Church* without Him : That He be underſtood as the *Principle* of *Unity* in His *Church* ; ſo that, they who unjuſtly break off from his *Communion*, are thereby in a *Schiſm* : That he ſhew his *Succeſſion*, by Regular Ordination, convey'd down from the *Apoſtles*. In ſhort, that He have all that *Character* and

I

Autho-

Authority, which we fee to have been Recogniz'd in the *Bishops*, in the very Age of the *Apostles*, and all the fucceeding Ages of *Christianity*; and then call Him *Moderator*, *Superintendent*, or *Bishop*: For, the Conteft is not about the *Name*, but the *Thing*.

And if we go only upon the *Etymology* of the *word*, how fhall we prove *Presbyters* to be an *Order* in the *Church*, more than *Bifhops*? as *Athanafius* faid to *Dracontius* of thofe who perfuaded him not to accept of a *Bifhoprick*.

why do they perfuade you not to be a Bifhop, when they themfelves will have Presbyters?	Διὰ τι συμβυλεύουσί σοι μὴ ἀντιλαμβάνεσθαι σε τῆς Ἐπισκοπῆς, αὐζοὶ θέλοντες ἔχειν πρεσβυτέρους;

I will end this Head, with the Advice of that great *Father* to this fame *Dracontius*.

If the Government of the Churches do not pleafe you; and that you think the Office of a *Bifhop* has no Reward, thereby making your felf a Defpifer of our *Saviour*, who did Inftitute it; I befeech you furmife not any fuch things as thefe, nor do you Entertain any who advife fuch things; for that is not worthy of *Dracontius*: For what things the Lord did Inftitute by His *Apoftles*, thofe things remain both good and fure.	Ἐι ὃ τῆς Ἐκκλησιῶν ἡ Διάταξις οὐκ ἀρέσκει σοι, οὐδὲ νομίζεις ὃ τῆς Ἐπισκοπῆς λειτούργημα μισθὸν ἔχειν, ἀλλὰ καταφρονεῖν τῷ ταῦτα διαταξαμένε Σωτῆρος πεποίηκας σαὐτὸν, ἀρακαλῶ, μὴ ζιαῦτα λογίζου, μηδὲ ἀνέχου τῶ ταῦτα συμβυλόόντων. ᾿ γὰ ἀξία Δεακοντίου ταῦτα. ἃ γὰ ὁ Κύρος διὰ τῆς Ἀπόλων πέπωκε, ζαῦτα καλὰ καὶ βέβαία μένε.

Athanaf. Epift. ad *Dracont.*

II. Having thus Explain'd thofe Texts of *Scripture* which fpeak of *Epifcopacy*, by the Concurrent fenfe of thofe who liv'd with the *Apoftles*, and were taught the Faith from their Mouths; who liv'd zealous *Confeffors*, and dy'd glorious *Martyrs* of *Chrift*; and who Succeeded the *Apoftles* in thofe very *Churches* where themfelves had fat *Bifhops*: And having deduc'd their Teftimonies, and of thofe who Succeeded them down for Four Hundred and Fifty Years after *Chrift* (from which time, ther is no doubt rais'd againft the Univerfal Reception of *Epifcopacy*) and this not only from their *Writings* apart, but by their *Canons* and *Laws*, when Affembl'd together in *Council*; which one wou'd think fufficient Evidence, againft none at all on the other fide, that is, for the *Succeffion* of

Churches

Churches in the *Presbyterian* Form, of which no one Inftance can be given, fo much as of any one *Church* in the *world* fo Deduc'd, not only from the days of the *Apoftles* (as is fhewn for *Epifcopacy*) but before *Calvin*, and thofe who *Reform'd* with him, about 160 Years laft paft: I fay, tho' what is done is fufficient to fatisfie any *Indifferent* and *Un-byafs'd* Judgment, yet ther is one *Topick* yet behind, which, with our *Diffenters*, weighs more than all *Fathers* and *Councils*; and that is, the late *Reformation*, from whence fome Date their very *Chriftianity*. And if even by this too *Epifcopacy* fhou'd be *witneffed* and *Approv'd*, then is ther nothing at all in the World left to the Oppofers of *Epifcopacy*, nothing of *Antiquity*, *Precedent*, or any *Authority* but their own *wilful will* againft all *Ages* of the whole *Catholick Church*, even that of the *Reformation* as well as all the Reft.

Let us then Examine. Firft, for the *Church* of *England*, that is thrown off clearly by our *Diffenters*, for that was *Reform'd* under *Epifcopacy*, and continues fo to this day.

And as to our Neighbour Nation of *Scotland*, where the *Presbyterians* do boaft that the *Reformation* was made by *Presbyters*; that is moft *clearly* and *Authentically* Confuted by a Late Learned and worthy Author (already mention'd) in his *Fundamental Charter of Presbytery*, Printed 1695. fo as to ftop the Mouths of the moft Perverfe, who will not be Perfuaded tho' they are Perfuaded.

Go we then abroad, and fee the ftate of the *Reformed* Churches there.

The *Lutherans* are all cut off, as the Church of *England*; for they ftill Retain *Epifcopacy*, as in *Denmark*, *Sweden*, &c.

Ther remains now only the *Calvinifts*. Here it is the *Presbyterians* fet up their Reft ! This is their ftrong *Foundation* !

And this will fail them as much as all the other: For, be it known unto them (however they will receive it) that *Calvin* himfelf, and *Beza*, and the reft of the Learned *Reformers* of their Part, did give their Teftimony for *Epifcopacy* as much as any. They counted it a moft unjuft *Reproach* upon them, to think that they condemn'd *Epifcopacy*; which they fay they did not throw off, but cou'd not have it there, in *Geneva*, without coming under the *Papal Hierarchy*: They highly *Applauded* and *Congratulated* the *Epifcopal Hierarchy* of the *Church* of *England*, as in their feve-

ral

ral Letters to Q. *Elizabeth*, to the *Arch-bishop* of *Canterbury*, and o-thers of our *English Bishops*: They Pray'd heartily to God for the Con-tinuance and Preservation of it : Bemoan'd their own unhappy Cir-cumstances, that they cou'd not have the like, because they had no *Magistrate* to Protect them ; and wished for *Episcopacy* in their *Church-es*, the want of which they own'd as a great *Defect* ; but call'd it their *Misfortune* rather than their *Fault*. As the Learned of the *French Hugonots* have likewise pleaded on their Behalf.

As for their *Excuse*. I do not now meddle with it, for I think it was not a good one. They might have had *Bishops* from other Places, tho' ther were none among themselves, but those who were *Popish*: And they might as well have had *Bishops* as *Presby-ters*, without the Countenance of the *Civil-Magistrate*. It might have rais'd a greater *Persecution* against them ; but that is nothing as to the *Truth* of the thing. And if they thought it a *Truth*, they ought to have *suffer'd* for it.

But whatever becomes of their *Excuse*, here it is plain, that they gave their *Suffrage* for *Episcopacy* ; which who so pleases may see at large in Dr. *Durel's View of the Government and Worship in the Refor-med Churches beyond the Seas*, (who was himself one of them) Printed. 1662.

So that our Modern *Presbyterians* have departed from *Calvin* as well as from *Luther*, in their Abhorrence of *Episcopacy*, from all the *Christian* World, in all Ages ; and particularly from all our late *Reformers*, both of one sort and other.

Calvin wou'd have *Anathematiz'd* all of them, had he liv'd in our times. He say's ther were none such to be found in his time, who oppos'd the *Episcopal Hierarchy*, but only the *Papal*, which As-pir'd to an *Universal Supremacy* in the *See* of *Rome* over the whole *Catholick Church*, which is the *Prerogative* of *Christ* alone. But, says he,

If they wou'd give us such a *Hierarchy*, in which the *Bishops* shou'd so Excell, as that they did not refuse to be subject to *Christ*, and to depend upon Him , as their *only* Head, and refer all to Him ; then I will confess that they are worthy of all *Ana-themas*, if any such shall be

Talem si nobis Hierarchiam ex-hibeant, in qua sic Emineant Epis-copi, *ut Christo subesse non Recu-sent, & ab Illo tanquam unico Capite pendeant, & ad Ipsum re-ferantur,* &c. *Tum vero nullo non Anathemate dignos fatear si qui erunt qui non Eam Reverean-tur, summaque Obedientia obser-*

found , who will not Reve- *vent. Galvin. De neceſſ.tat. Ec-*
rence it, and ſubmit themſelves *claſ. Reformand.*
to it, with the utmoſt Obedience.

See, he ſays; *ſi qui erunt,* if ther ſhall be any ſuch, which ſuppoſes
that he knew none ſuch ; and that he own'd none ſuch amongſt his
Reformers : And that if ever any ſuch thou'd ariſe, he thought ther
were no *Anathemas* which they did not deſerve, who ſhou'd refuſe
to ſubmit to the *Epiſcopal Hierarchy,* without ſuch an *Univerſal
Head,* as Excludes *Chriſt* from being the *only* Univerſal *Head* ; for
if ther be *another,* (tho *ſubſtitute*) He is not *only.* Thus He is called
the *Chief Biſhop,* but never the *only Biſhop,* becauſe ther are others
deputed under Him. But He calls no *Biſhop* the *Univerſal Biſhop,*
or *Head* of the *Catholick Church,* becauſe He has appointed no *Sub-
ſtitute* in that ſupreme Office ; as not of *Univerſal King,* ſo neither of *Univerſal Biſhop.*

And *Beza* ſuppoſes as Poſitively as *Calvin* had done, that ther
were none who did oppoſe the *Epiſcopal Hierarchy* without ſuch an
Univerſal Head now upon Earth ; or that oppos'd the *Order* of *Epiſcopacy* ; and condemns them as *Mad-men,* if any ſuch cou'd be
found. For thus ſays he,

If ther be any (which you ｜*Si qui ſunt autem (quod ſane mihi
ſhall hardly peſwade me to be- ｜non facile perſuaſeris) qui omnem
lieve) who reject the whole ｜Epiſcoporum ordinem Rejiciant, ab-
Order of *Epiſcopacy,* God forbid ｜ſit ut quiſquam ſatis ſanæ mentis
that any Man, in his wits, ｜furoribus illorum aſſentiatur.Bez.1.
ſhou'd aſſent to the *Madneſs* of ｜ad Tractat.de Miniſtr.Ev.Grad.ab
ſuch Men. ｜Hadrian.Sarav. Belga Editam.c.1.*

And particularly as to the *Church* of *England,* and her *Hierarchy* of *Archbiſhops* and *Biſhops,* he ſays, that he never meant to op-
pugne any thing of that ; but calls it a *ſingular Bleſſing of God* ;
and *wiſhes that ſhe may ever en-* ｜*Fruatur ſane iſta ſingulari Dei
joy it.* ｜beneficentia, quæ utinam ſit illi
｜Perpetua.* Ibid. c. 18.

So that our Modern *Presbyterians* are diſarm'd of the Precedent
of *Calvin, Beza,* and all the *Reformers* abroad ; by whoſe Sentence
they are *Anathematiz'd,* and counted as *Mad-men.*

Here then, let us conſider and beware of the Fatal Progreſs of
Error ! *Calvin* and the *Reformers* with him, ſet up *Presbyterian* Go-
vernment, as they pretended, by *Neceſſity* ; but ſtill kept up and
Pro-

Profeſs'd the higheſt Regard to the *Epiſcopal Charaƈter* and *Authority* : But thoſe who pretend to follow their Example, have utterly Abdicated the whole *Order* of *Epiſcopacy,* as *Anti-Chriſtian* and an *Inſupportable Grievance* ! While, at the ſame time, they wou'd ſeem to pay the greateſt Reverence to theſe *Reformers* ; and much more to the *Authority* of the *Firſt* and *Pureſt* Ages of *Chriſtianity* ; whoſe *Fathers* and *Councils* ſpoke all the *High* things, before Quoted, in behalf of *Epiſcopacy* ; far beyond the *Language* of our later *Apologiſts* for that *Hierarchy* ; or what durſt now be Repeated, except from ſuch *unqueſtionable Authority.*

In this they imitate the hardneſs of the *Jews,* who Built the *Sepulchers* of thoſe *Prophets,* whom their *Fathers* ſlew ; while, at the ſame time, they Adher'd to, and out-did the Wickedneſs of their *Fathers,* in Perſecuting the *Succeſſors* of thoſe *Prophets.*

F I N I S.

E R R A T A.

Pag. 3. col. 2. l. 11. r. κοιμηθῶσιν. P. 39. col. 1. l. 10, 11. r. All of you follow your Biſhops. col. 2. penult. r. ἐὰν. p. 40. l. 16. A. D. 180. ſhou'd be on the Margent ; p. 42. col. 2. l. 3. dele—— after Πρεσβυτέρων. and r. ἐρεῖς. p. 44. col. 2. l. 14. r. Ira. p 45. col. 2. l. 28. r. ſcripturarum. p. 47. col. 2. penult. r. ad Heliodorum. p. 51. col. 1. l. 11, 12, 13, 14. r. As likewiſe ſuch other *Clergy,* and as many as ſhall join with him : but the *Lay-men* ſhall be Excommunicated.

ADVERTISEMENT.

WHereas I have plac'd the *Apoftolical Canons* in the Front of the *Councils* before Quoted, I thought fit (to prevent needlefs Cavil) to give this Advertifement, that I do not contend, they were made by the *Apoftles* themfelves; but by the Holy *Fathers* of the *Church*, about the end of the *Second* and beginning of the *Third Century*, as a *Summary* of that *Difcipline*, which had been tranfmitted to them, by Un-interrupted Tradition, from the *Apoftles*; whence they have juftly obtain'd the Name of *The Apoftolical Canons*; and, as fuch, have been Receiv'd, and Reverenc'd in the fucceeding Ages of Chriftianity.

The *Councils* Quoted after thefe *Canons*, bear their Proper Dates; and ther can be no. Conteft about them.

And what is Quoted of St. *Ignatius* and the other *Fathers*, is from the moft Uncontroverted Parts of their Works, to obviate the Objection of *Interpolations*, and *Additions*, by the Noife of which our Adverfaries endeavour to throw off, or enervate their whole Authority; and quite to dif-arm us of all that *Light* which we have from the *Primitive Ages* of the *Church*; becaufe it makes all againft them. Though they fail not to Quote the *Fathers* on their fide, whenfoever they can Screw them to give the leaft feeming Countenance to their *Novelties* and Errors: Yet *Boldly* Reject them All, when brought in Evidence againft them; and that they can no otherwife ftruggle from under the weight of their Authority.

Some Seafonable Reflections upon the Quakers Solemn Pro-teftation againft *George Keith*'s Proceedings at *Turner's-Hall*, 29. *April* 1697. Which was by them Printed, and fent thither, as the Reafons of their not Appearing to defend themfelves. Herein annex'd Verbatim By an Impartial Hand.

Satan Dif-rob'd from his Difguife of Light: Or, the Quakers Laft Shift to Cover their Monftrous Herefies, laid fully o-pen. In a Reply to *Thomas Ellwood*'s Anfwer (Publifhed the End of laft Month) to *George Keith*'s Narrative of the Proceedings at *Turner's-Hall*, *June* 11. 1696. Which alfo may ferve for a Reply (as to the main Points of Doctrine) to *Geo. white-head*'s Anfwer to The Snake in the Grafs; to be Publifhed the End of next Month, if this prevent it not.

A Difcourfe proving the Divine Inftitution of Water-Bap-tifm: Wherein the Quaker-Arguments againft it; are Collected and Confuted. With as much as is needful concerning the Lord's Supper. Thefe Four Books are Written by the Author of The Snake in the Grafs.

The Quakers fet in their True Light, in order to give the Nation a clear fight of what they hold concerning Jefus of *Nazareth*, the Scriptures, Water-Baptifm, the Lord's Supper, Magiftracy, Miniftry, Laws, and Government: Hiftorically-col-lected out of their moft approved Authors, which are their beft Conftruing-Books, from the year of their Rife 1650, to the year of their Progrefs 1696. By *Francis Bugg*, Sen.

An Effay concerning Preaching: Written for the Direction of a Young Divine; and ufeful alfo for the People, in order to Profitable Hearing.

Crums of Comfort, and Godly Prayers; With Thankful Remembrances of God's wonderful Deliverances of this Land.